FASTING

STUDENT EDITION

JENTEZEN
FRANKLIN

FASTING
STUDENT EDITION

PASSIO

Most CHARISMA HOUSE BOOK GROUP products are available at special quantity discounts for bulk purchase for sales promotions, premiums, fund-raising, and educational needs. For details, write Charisma House Book Group, 600 Rinehart Road, Lake Mary, Florida 32746, or telephone (407) 333-0600.

FASTING: STUDENT EDITION by Jentezen Franklin
Published by Passio
Charisma Media/Charisma House Book Group
600 Rinehart Road
Lake Mary, Florida 32746
www.charismahouse.com

Unless otherwise noted, all Scripture quotations are from the New King James Version of the Bible. Copyright © 1979, 1980, 1982 by Thomas Nelson, Inc., publishers. Used by permission.

Scripture quotations marked AMP are from the Amplified Bible. Old Testament copyright © 1965, 1987 by the Zondervan Corporation. The Amplified New Testament copyright © 1954, 1958, 1987 by the Lockman Foundation. Used by permission.

Scripture quotations marked NAS are from the New American Standard Bible, Copyright © 1960, 1962, 1963, 1968, 1971, 1972, 1973, 1975, 1977, 1995 by The Lockman Foundation. Used by permission. (www.Lockman.org)

Scripture quotations marked NIV are from the Holy Bible, New International Version of the Bible. Copyright © 1973, 1978, 1984, International Bible Society. Used by permission.

Cover design by Justin Evans
Design Director: Bill Johnson

Visit the author's website at www.jentezenfranklin.org.

Library of Congress Control Number: 2012907524
International Standard Book Number: 978-1-61638-852-2
E-book ISBN: 978-1-62136-043-8

This book is adapted from *Fasting*, published by Charisma House, ISBN 978-1-59979-258-3, copyright © 2008.

12 13 14 15 16 — 9 8 7 6 5 4 3 2 1
Printed in the United States of America

To my five children—Courteney, Caressa, Caroline, Connar, and Drake—and everyone who shares in the destiny of the next generation. You will face great challenges, but God is greater. As you make fasting and seeking God a part of your life, I rejoice in anticipation of all that God will do through you to change the world.

Contents

SECTION 1

The Private Discipline That Brings Public Reward

Blessed are those who hunger and thirst for righteousness, for they shall be filled.

—Matthew 5:6

Introduction

What's Your Secret?

ONE OF MY favorite questions to ask older men and women in the faith whom I admire is, "What's your secret?" This is a great question to ask if you genuinely desire deeper intimacy with the Lord and knowledge of God's perfect will. Over the years I've heard all kinds of answers, and other people's wisdom has helped me grow to know, love, and serve God better.

But someone recently asked *me* the question. I didn't even pause before I answered with one powerful word: fasting.

For me fasting has been the secret to obtaining open doors, miraculous provision, favor, and the tender touch of God upon my life. I was on a three-day fast when He called me to preach. I was on a twenty-one-day fast when our ministry received its first million-dollar gift. When I was an evangelist, my brother and I traveled together and would rotate our preaching nights. On my night off I would fast all day for him. On his night off he fasted all day for me. We went from obscurity to doors opening for us all over the world. Every assignment has a launching pad. When God has placed a dream inside you that only He can make possible, you need to fast and pray.

Now that I'm a pastor, our church begins each year with a twenty-one-day fast. From those early years of ministry until this day, fasting has become a lifestyle. When I feel myself growing dry spiritually, when I don't sense that cutting-edge anointing, or when I need a fresh encounter with God, fasting is the secret key that unlocks heaven's door and slams shut the gates of hell.

The discipline of fasting releases the anointing, the favor, and the blessing of God in the life of a Christian. As you read this book, I'll show you the power of the threefold cord. I'll show you how every major biblical character fasted. I will teach you how to fast. Most importantly, as you read this book, you are going to develop a hunger to fast. I don't know about you, but there are some things that I desire more than food. "Blessed are those who hunger and thirst for righteousness, for they shall be filled" (Matt. 5:6).

Since you're reading this book, you probably are not content to go through this year the same way you went through last year. You know there's more. You know there's an assignment for your life. You know there are things God desires to release in your life, and there is a genuine desperation for those things gripping your heart. It was for you, and for those like you, that this book was written. Now I want to invite you to join this marvelous journey.

Chapter 1

Fasting—a Source of Hidden Power

A RE YOU LOOKING for a more vibrant and meaningful relationship with God? Have you ever wanted to experience God in a way that knocks your socks off or takes your breath away?

What's *a-m-a-z-i-n-g* about God is that no matter how much you long or ache for Him, He desires a relationship with you even more! In His radical love God provides lots of ways for you to experience and know Him more—through studying Scripture, through prayer, through growing in Christian community, and through surrounding yourselves with friends who love God with a mighty passion.

But He provides another way you can grow spiritually that people don't like to talk about as often: fasting.

Why don't people talk about ultrapowerful, life-changing spiritual activity more? Maybe it's because of the reaction. Too often people begin to stress out or roll their eyes or even pull a U-turn when they see the word *fasting*. You might even be one of them.

Let's be honest. Fasting stirs up all kinds of colorful pictures and ideas—a ton of which are based on misunderstandings and misconceptions. Some people think fasting is simply skipping a meal or two. Others think of fasting as a diet plan, a quick way to shave off a few pounds so they can get back into their skinny jeans. Others think of fasting as something done by only the hard-core super Christians or some hooded religious monks who live in a cave in the middle of no man's land in the desert.

But fasting is so much more. Fasting is a personal invitation from God to grow deeper in your relationship with Him and experience His presence more fully in your life. Fasting, according to the Bible, is meant to be a normal part of your relationship with God—not just something saved for special people or special occasions.

Biblical fasting invites you to refrain from food for a spiritual purpose. In the Old Testament we read about a young shepherd boy named David. The youngest of his brothers, he was the least likely to be selected to do anything special. A prophet by the name of Samuel visited the family one day and announced that David had been chosen by God to be the future king of Israel. Everyone's jaws fell open in astonishment. Who was this rascal of a little brother? Why would God choose him?

> "As the deer pants for the water brooks, so pants my soul for You, O God. My soul thirsts for God, for the living God. When shall I come and appear before God? My tears have been my food day and night, while they continually say to me, 'Where is your God?'" —Psalm 42:1–3

David turned out to be one of the most remarkable kings in the history of Israel. Not only did he courageously fight countless battles and become the hero of his nation, but he also kept growing and pursuing God throughout his lifetime. One of the great hallmarks of David's life was that he was described as "a man after God's own heart." He pursued the Lord with everything—praying, studying, worshiping, and seeking to grow in his relationship with the Lord. But if you look at his story, you'll discover that fasting also marked David's life. And the practice of fasting took him further and deeper in his relationship with God than he could have ever imagined!

In Psalm 42:7 David describes a deep spiritual longing that developed between himself and God. He described it as, "Deep calls unto deep." David discovered the spiritual truth that fasting ushers us into a more intimate and powerful relationship with the Lord.

David lived a radical life for God, and so can you! When you eliminate food from your diet for a period of time, something amazing happens in your life: your spirit becomes uncluttered by the things of this world and amazingly sensitive to the things of God. You become hyperaware of the Lord's presence and notice Him in situations and events you may have never seen Him in before.

Though it may seem like upside-down thinking, fasting ignites your passion for God so that your hunger and thirst for Him are *greater* than your natural desire for food. Imagine that! Through fasting you can reach a place where you're able to cry out from the depths of your spirit to the depths of God.

Once you've experienced even a glimpse of this kind of intimacy with our God—your Father, the holy Creator of the universe—and the countless rewards and blessings that follow, you can't help but want more. Fasting stirs your hunger for God. As you begin the adventure of fasting in your spiritual journey, you'll find your whole perspective will change as you discover fasting as a secret source of power that's available to you—yes, you!—as a child of God.

A THREEFOLD CORD

Have you ever looked closely at someone's braid? Maybe on a lazy afternoon you've braided your friend's hair, or maybe you've been courageous enough to let her braid yours. If you look closely at the braid, you can follow the strands to see how each piece of hair lines up to be woven together.

Imagine tugging on someone's braid. How do you think the person would respond? You might hear a yell or feel your hand being shoved away, or worse!

Now imagine just tugging on an individual strand of hair. How do you think the person would respond?

You might hear a small yelp or be asked to stop, but the response probably wouldn't be as strong. In the end you'd likely be holding a stray hair in your hand.

That's a glimpse into the power of a threefold cord. You can easily pull a single strand of hair out of your or your sibling's head. But when hair is woven together, the braid is stronger, making it much more difficult to remove.

In the same way, you may be able to take a pair of scissors and cut through a single cord. But if you have three cords and weave them together, cutting through them is much more difficult—if not impossible. Solomon, when writing the books of wisdom for Israel, noted that a cord, or rope, braided with three strands is strong.

> A threefold cord is not quickly broken.
>
> —ECCLESIASTES 4:12

I can't help but think that Jesus had this passage in mind as He taught. In the years that He walked the earth, Jesus devoted time to teaching His disciples principles of the kingdom of

God, principles that conflict with those of this world. In the Beatitudes, specifically in Matthew 6, Jesus provided the pattern by which each of us is to live as a child of God. That pattern addressed three specific duties of a Christian: giving, praying, and fasting. Jesus said, "*When* you give ..." and "*When* you pray ..." and "*When* you fast ..." He made it clear that fasting, like giving and praying, was a normal part of Christian life. As much attention should be given to fasting as to giving and praying.

Likewise, when giving, praying, and fasting are practiced together in your life, it creates a type of threefold cord that is not easily broken. You'll find yourself strengthened and impassioned—becoming a source of encouragement to your friends.

You'll also find that in some of the areas in your life where you've been waiting on God—your family, your relationships, your classes, your workplace—you finally receive a breakthrough.

The Gospel of Matthew tells the story of a father who had a demon-possessed son. For years this father watched helplessly as his son suffered with severe convulsions. As the son grew older, the attacks became so severe that he would often throw himself into an open fire or a trench of water. A suicidal spirit tormented him constantly, and the situation became life threatening.

The boy's dad tried everything he could think of, but nothing worked. He felt so discouraged and defeated. Then he heard that Jesus and His disciples were near. At first, he approached the disciples, but they were clueless about how to cure the boy. Then, going to the Master, he cried for mercy. He explained that his son was out of his mind and tormented.

Jesus didn't hesitate. He instructed the father to bring his son. When the boy was brought to Jesus, the Bible says Jesus rebuked the evil spirit, and it immediately left. The child was cured in that moment. But what made the difference? After all, Matthew 10:1 records that Jesus had already given the disciples power to cast out evil spirits and to heal every disease. So why couldn't the disciples cast out the demon and cure the boy?

That's what they wanted to know too. So later that night, when they were alone with Jesus, they asked Him. Matthew goes on to tell us Jesus replied, "Because of your unbelief; for assuredly, I say to you, if you have faith as a mustard seed, you will say to this mountain, 'Move from here to there,' and it will move; and nothing will be impossible for you. However, this kind does not go out except by prayer and fasting" (Matt. 17:20–21).

I've read the passage many times and even taught from it on occasion. But each time I've focused on the statement "and nothing will be impossible for you." I think a lot of people stop right there, but Jesus didn't because He knew there was more—much more.

See, that funny little word *however* is the connection—it's the key that unlocks the power in the statement "nothing will be impossible for you." Jesus told the disciples they needed faith, even faith the size of a tiny seed. But that wasn't all. Long before this incident the Holy Spirit led Jesus into the wilderness, where He spent forty days and forty nights while taking no food. For Jesus, casting out that stubborn evil spirit wasn't impossible.

If Jesus could have accomplished all He came to do without fasting, why would He fast? The Son of God fasted because He knew there were supernatural things that could only be released this way. How much more should fasting be a common practice in our lives?

FASTING IS FOR EVERYONE

Perhaps you're thinking, "I still don't know how fasting can really be for me." Maybe you discount yourself because of your age, or the length of time you've been following Jesus, or your affection for fresh, thick-crust pizza. While you may try to disqualify yourself from fasting, Jesus called those who follow Him to fasting.

Now you may be thinking that Jesus's actual disciples, the twelve followers who journeyed with Him, didn't fast. But if you look at the Bible, you'll find Jesus's response. When addressing the Pharisees as to why His disciples did not fast, Jesus replied, "Can you make the friends of the bridegroom fast while the bridegroom is with them? But the days will

> "A disciple is not above his teacher, but everyone who is perfectly trained will be like his teacher."
> —Luke 6:40

come when the bridegroom will be taken away from them; *then they will fast* in those days" (Luke 5:34–35, emphasis added).

Notice how Jesus responded: *Then they will fast.* Though the disciples didn't fast while they were with Jesus, they did fast after He died and was resurrected. But Jesus's words weren't just for His immediate disciples but for all His disciples—including you and me.

I find great comfort in knowing that Jesus didn't expect His disciples to do something He hadn't done as well. Remember that before the Lord ever launched into ministry, He spent forty days fasting. Jesus isn't calling us to the impossible in fasting—but He shows us that all things are possible through Him.

The great news is that fasting isn't just about what you're giving up—food—but it's also about what you're gaining in your relationship with God. In fact, God delights in rewarding and revealing Himself to those who seek Him.

> "Then Jesus, being filled with the Holy Spirit, returned from the Jordan and was led by the Spirit into the wilderness, being tempted for forty days by the devil. And in those days He ate nothing, and afterward, when they had ended, He was hungry." —Luke 4:1–2

In the Old Testament we read an incredible story of one young man who was wildly rewarded for passionate pursuit of God through prayer and fasting. Daniel was taken away from his homeland and grew up in Babylon among a people and nation that was foreign to him. Not only was the culture strange to him, but also the Babylonians didn't worship or love God. Yet Daniel chose to continue pursuing Him, and though he lived in Babylonian captivity, his fasting—even partial fasting of certain foods—brought about the open reward of God, who blessed Daniel with wisdom beyond that of anyone else in that empire.

If you read the amazing book of Daniel, you'll discover that at another point he was grieved and burdened with the revelation he had received for Israel. In response Daniel ate no choice breads or meats and drank no wine for three weeks. Then he described the angel that was sent to him—which had been *delayed* by the prince of Persia for twenty-one days—with the answers Daniel sought. His fast broke the power of the delayer and released the angels of God so that His purposes could be revealed and served.

God rewards those who seek Him—and one of the best ways to pursue the Lord is through prayer and fasting. Why combine fasting with prayer? Because you probably have areas in your life right now where you really need to hear from God and experience a breakthrough.

Maybe you're struggling with school or with a particular coach or teacher.

Maybe you're wondering what God has for you after graduation or in your career.

Maybe you're trying to figure out if the person you're dating is "the one."

Maybe you're struggling with a critical decision that you know is going to shape the rest of your life.

In the upcoming pages you'll learn how fasting brings you to a place of being able to more clearly hear God's voice and walk in the center of His will. Whether you desire to be closer to God or are in need of a great breakthrough in your life, remember that nothing shall be impossible to you. Fasting is truly a secret source of power!

King Stomach's Reign

I F FASTING IS a source of secret power and gives us an opportunity to grow more passionate for God, then why don't more people fast? Why isn't fasting more popular in churches, schools, and on college campuses around our nation? When it comes to the threefold cord, prayer is celebrated and giving is encouraged, but fasting? Well, it's just not talked about that often.

If the threefold cord of Christian duties were praying, giving, and *shopping*, or praying, giving, and *playing Xbox*, I think the third fold of the cord would be a lot more popular. But God calls us to fasting—to abstain from food. We're invited to give up our own pleasures and desires in order to pursue Him. So as part of the threefold cord of normal Christian duties, why is fasting so often overlooked?

Let's be honest: fasting isn't easy.

Fasting asks us to overcome all the temptations and the taunts of someone I like to call "King Stomach." If you don't know King Stomach, just slide this book out of the way, look down at your belly button, and introduce yourself. (Beware of any lint you may find.) There's a chance King Stomach has already been making noise—rumbling and grumbling—as you've been reading this book. King Stomach doesn't keep desire to himself. He lets you know whenever he starts to empty by reminding you to eat—and eat now!

Our stomachs play an important role in each of our lives. A healthy hunger level reminds us to consume the calories we need to play sports, think creatively, and live vibrant lives. And food is one of the great gifts of God. It's something meant to be enjoyed and provide the nourishment we need—not just to survive, but thrive.

The problem begins when our stomachs become the kings of our lives—controlling us by demanding that we eat in response to everything from a moment of boredom to a shift in our moods. If left unchecked, King Stomach will demand that you eat when you're happy, sad, mad, and feeling bad. King Stomach will tell you to eat when you're busy and when you're bored, when you're alone and when you're with others. King Stomach will tell you that the solution to every challenge you face is food. King Stomach rules like a dictator, telling us that no matter what the situation is, we need to "Eat, eat, eat!"

This is one of the big reasons why fasting is so important: it dethrones King Stomach.

When you first try to fast—even if it's just for a meal or half a day—you're going to hear King Stomach crying out louder than before, "Eat, eat, eat!" But when you fast, you'll discover something amazing happens. Not only will God give you the grace and strength to fast as you seek Him, but also King Stomach's voice will start to fade. Through fasting, King Stomach is dethroned so you can more clearly hear the voice of God in your life.

AN AGE-OLD BATTLEGROUND

This battle of dethroning King Stomach isn't anything new. It's been around since the beginning of time. The Bible shows us countless stories of what happens when King Stomach gets his way.

The call to "Eat, eat, eat!" traces all the way to the Garden of Eden. The Book of Genesis records that God planted a garden in Eden. He created a man and woman named Adam and Eve, whose responsibility was to care for the garden.

The Bible says, "The LORD God planted a garden eastward in Eden, and there He put the man whom He had formed. And out of the ground the LORD God made every tree grow that is pleasant to the sight and good for food" (Gen. 2:8–9).

Now the plants God created in the garden weren't just beautiful; they were also a source of food. So God designed people from the beginning to enjoy food. The first couple was given permission to eat of any tree in the garden and encouraged to enjoy the food freely. Imagine for a moment what it was like walking through the garden eating all kinds of fruits—sweet and sour and tangy—along with wild berries and grapes for the very first time. I can imagine Eve picking a pear and saying to Adam, "Oooh, you've got to try this one!"

But God gave very specific instructions regarding one lone tree in the garden. He said that the first couple could eat from any tree —every fruit in sight was fair game—except for one. The tree of the knowledge of good and evil was off limits. That was the one tree in the whole garden the first couple was forbidden from eating, because if they took a bite they would die.

The problem came when the man and woman disobeyed God's instruction. A crafty serpent approached Eve and suggested that if she ate of the forbidden fruit, she wouldn't really die. In essence the snake convinced Eve that God didn't really mean what He said. As she held the fruit in her hand, I bet she could hear the rumbling of King Stomach.

The Bible says, "So when the woman saw that the tree was good for food, that it was pleasant to the eyes, and a tree desirable to make one wise, she took of its fruit and ate. She also gave to her husband with her, and he ate" (Gen. 3:6).

Adam's and Eve's appetites got the best of them. They gave in to King Stomach, and in a flash they lost everything. The couple went from peacefully enjoying God's presence in the coolness of the garden to fearfully hiding from Him among the trees.

They literally ate themselves out of house and home. They ate themselves out of the will of God for their lives. They ate themselves out of God's provision and out of His magnificent presence. Though their stomachs were temporarily satisfied, we still suffer the consequences of their appetites today.

WHEN APPETITE REIGNS

Adam and Eve aren't the only ones who gave in to their appetites and allowed King Stomach to get the best of them. They were just the first. Later on in the Book of Genesis we read about Sodom and Gomorrah—two cities famed for their sinfulness. These places were so sinful that they were destroyed. When people talk about the sins of Sodom and Gomorrah, they often focus on the rampant homosexuality in those cities. But that's not all the Bible teaches.

Tucked away in the Book of Ezekiel is a deeper insight into what was really going on in those cities. Scripture tells us, "Look, this was the iniquity of your sister Sodom: She and her daughter had pride, fullness of food, and abundance of idleness;

neither did she strengthen the hand of the poor and needy. And they were haughty and committed abomination before Me; therefore I took them away as I saw fit" (Ezek. 16:49–50).

Remember the threefold cord? If you look at this passage, you'll see that no one in these cities were giving to the poor and needy or praying, as noted by the abundance of pride and idleness. Now consider the third cord. The people in these towns were also guilty of gluttony (fullness of food). In other words, they ate too much. They allowed the cries of King Stomach to rule in their lives until all they cared about was themselves.

We live in a day and age when a lot of people are raising the issues of social justice and caring for the poor. I'm a huge fan of both. But we need to recognize that caring for others and giving voice to those who have no voice begins in our own hearts. To be sensitive to the leading of God's Spirit in our lives and live passionately for Him, we need to make sure that Jesus is the true King in our lives—not our stomachs.

One of the most compelling stories about the power of appetite derailing someone's life is the story of Esau. As the oldest son of Isaac and Rebekah, Esau would receive his father's birthright and blessing. He also would get a double portion of his father's estate. These were both tangible and intangible gifts that were not to be taken lightly.

Now Esau loved food. He savored anything you could cook on the grill. One day Esau returned from hunting empty-handed and with a killer appetite. I have a hunch that King Stomach was kicking and screaming inside Esau on that day. When Esau walked into the tent of his brother, Jacob, he caught a whiff of food. Then he saw a simple meal of lentils and bread prepared and waiting to be eaten. His stomach roared. Esau begged Jacob for the food.

Recognizing that King Stomach was ruling in Esau's life,

Jacob knew he could take advantage of his brother. So he negotiated a deal: a meal in exchange for the birthright and blessing. A business student with even a C average could tell you the deal was terrible. Who would trade a so-so meal for a double portion of the family inheritance and the blessing of God?

Then we read one of the saddest passages in the Bible, "And Jacob gave Esau bread and stew of lentils; then he ate and drank, arose, and went his way. Thus Esau despised his birthright" (Gen. 25:34).

In the moment Esau didn't pause and didn't look back. He didn't even seem to think twice about the bad deal he made. Esau sold his coveted birthright because of his allegiance to King Stomach. God had a plan, a destiny, a will for Esau's life, but Esau's craving for food and his desire for instant gratification ruled the day.

The writer of Hebrews used strong terms to warn against becoming like Esau: "[Look] diligently lest anyone fall short of the grace of God; lest any root of bitterness springing up cause trouble, and by this many become defiled; lest there be any fornicator or profane person like Esau, who for one morsel of food sold his birthright. For you know that afterward, when he wanted to inherit the blessing, he was rejected, for he found no place for repentance, though he sought it diligently with tears" (Heb. 12:15–17).

Esau's story reminds us that King Stomach doesn't have our best interests in mind. King Stomach tells us that appetite is more important than anything and everything—including our futures and inheritances as children of God.

King Stomach makes appearances throughout the Bible. Another of his more notable ones is in the story of the Israelites. These were God's people who lived for four hundred years under oppressive slavery in Egypt. God raised up a man by the name of Moses to speak out against the wicked rule of Pharaoh. Through a series of miracles in the land and sky, God's people were eventually set free.

As the Israelites left Egypt, they found themselves pinned against the Red Sea with Pharaoh's army chasing them down. God miraculously parted the Red Sea so the Israelites could make their way across and travel on to the Promised Land. Along the way God provided for their every need, even feeding them bread from heaven daily. This bread was called "manna," meaning "What is it?" The heavenly provision provided such a perfectly balanced diet that there was not one sick or feeble person among them for forty years—with no doctors, drugstores, or hospitals. Manna filled their bellies and kept their bodies healthy and strong. But even with such gracious provision, a grumbling began in their bellies and overcame their hearts.

The Bible tells us that the people developed an intense craving for the food of Egypt. They cried out for meat to eat. They reminisced about all the food they had in Egypt—the cucumbers, the melons, the leeks, the onions, and the garlic. They complained that all they had to eat was the bread from heaven.

> "Those who are under the power of a carnal mind, will have their lusts fulfilled, though it be to the certain damage and ruin of their precious souls." —Matthew Henry, commentator[1]

God heard their murmuring and complaining. As any mom can attest, it's not a good idea to get the cook mad at you. God said, "Therefore the LORD will give you meat, and you shall eat. You shall eat, not one day, nor two days, nor five days, nor ten days, nor twenty days, but for a whole month, until it comes out of your nostrils and becomes loathsome to you, because you have despised the LORD who is among you, and have wept before Him, saying, 'Why did we ever come up out of Egypt?'" (Num. 11:18–20).

Then God sent them quail in such a great abundance they stacked it two and a half feet deep. That's not a buffet; that's a feeding trough. King Stomach growled, "Eat, eat, eat!" and they ate, ate, ate! With meat still in their mouths, thousands of them died and were buried there. The place became known as Kibroth Hattaavah, which means "The Graves of Lusters," as a memorial to those who ate themselves right out of the Promised Land (Num. 11:34).

> "I have not departed from the commandment of His lips; I have treasured the words of His mouth more than my necessary food." —Job 23:12

The Israelites were given a Promised Land, and as children of God we also have a land full of promises He wants to give us. In fact, the Bible is jam-packed with amazing promises. These are divine promises about your purpose, your future, and the role you're meant to play in this generation. But some of them won't be realized if you allow King Stomach to rule your appetite and control your life.

The good news is that you can choose to dethrone King Stomach in your life simply by choosing to fast. Now there's always a reason not to start a fast. A birthday. A holiday. A vacation. A camping trip. A lunch date. A night at the movies. There's always something on the calendar that can cause us to talk ourselves out of taking the first step. But that first step is huge! If you'll just courageously take it and commit to skip a meal or maybe even a whole day's worth of meals, you'll be amazed at how God will show up. I'm a huge fan of fasting at the beginning of the year. Why? By doing so, you set the course for the rest of the year. Just as beginning your day with prayer sets the course for the rest of the day and covers anything that may happen, the same is true of beginning the year with a fast. You establish the course for the entire year by what you do with those first few days of each new year.

God wants us to give Him not only our best but also our first. You can carry that even further to give God the first part of every day, the first day of every week, the first portion of every dollar, and the first consideration in every decision. When you start off a year with fasting, you're giving God your first—literally. What's amazing is how often, when I've fasted at the beginning of the year, I experience God's presence and blessings in my life in greater measure throughout the rest of the year.

But you don't need to wait until next January to begin fasting. You can begin this week. You can choose to say no to King Stomach and your appetite in order to say yes to God through prayer and fasting. You can choose to set apart a portion of a day or even an entire day to seek the Lord through prayer and fasting. Tell God that you want Him to be on the throne of your heart, your life, and your stomach. Ask God to give you the grace and strength to fast. And be expectant for how He will work in you and through you.

Chapter 3

But How Do I Fast?

THE BIBLE HAS lots of stories of people—including Adam and Eve, the citizens of Sodom and Gomorrah, Esau, and the Israelites—who allowed King Stomach's rumbling to distract them from God's purposes. But the Bible is also full of marvelous stories of those who overcame the cries of King Stomach and listened to God instead.

Remember Moses, the guy selected by God to set the Israelites free from Pharaoh? Even after God's people left Egypt, Moses continued to seek the Lord through prayer and fasting. In fact, while on a forty-day fast Moses received the Ten Commandments (Exod. 34:27–28). These ten loving commands of God have shaped every generation since they were entrusted to Moses. Fasting played a key role in preparing Moses to hear from the Lord.

Men like Moses aren't the only ones who used fasting as a spiritual discipline to lean toward God to hear His voice and will. Many years later, under King Ahasuerus's reign, a beautiful woman turned to fasting at a crucial time in the history of God's people.

In a fit of rage King Ahasuerus dethroned the queen and needed to find a replacement. In order to find the best candidate, the king decided to hold a beauty pageant. A Jewish girl by the name of Esther won the competition as well as the king's heart. Meanwhile an evil leader by the name of Haman ordered the annihilation and plunder of all the Jews. The plan seems inconceivable, but when Esther learned of the horrible plot, she knew it was true. With the support of her Jewish cousin Mordecai, she called all the Jews in her city to join her for a three-day fast. As a result the Jews were spared, Haman's vile (which, if you rearrange the letters, also spells *evil*) plan was exposed, and he was hanged on the very gallows he built to destroy Mordecai. You can read more of the details of this amazing story about the power of prayer and fasting in Esther 4–7.

Another great example is in the story of Jehoshaphat, king of Judah. This God-fearing leader found himself surrounded by a powerful enemy army. He and his people were going to be decimated without the Lord's intervention. Scripture records that Jehoshaphat responded by setting himself apart to seek God. He even went as far as to proclaim a fast throughout all Judah. Everyone—from the children to the wives to the grandparents—sought the Lord together.

The young and old desperately needed to know the Lord's plan to defeat this great army. In the midst of the assembly of fasting people God spoke through a prophet who encouraged them, saying they shouldn't be afraid or discouraged. The battle was not theirs to fight. The battle belonged to God alone: "You will not need to fight in this battle. Position yourselves, stand still and see the salvation of the LORD, who is with you, O Judah and Jerusalem!' Do not fear or be dismayed; tomorrow go out against them, for the LORD is with you" (2 Chron. 20:17).

In the midst of the whole assembly God told Judah exactly how that enemy army would approach and exactly what they were to do in response: nothing but stand and watch. They gave tremendous praise to the Lord, who set ambushes against the enemy and defeated them. None escaped. When the people of Judah arrived, it took them three whole days to carry away the treasures.

The people didn't even have to fight because God fought for them. The battle took one day, and the Lord not only delivered them, but He also prospered them.

One of my favorite fasting stories is of Hannah, who was overcome with sadness because she couldn't have a baby. Yet she entrusted herself to God as she wept and refused to eat. God heard her prayers, and Hannah soon had a bouncing baby boy. But not just any child; she gave birth to the great prophet Samuel.

When you start looking in the Bible for fasting, you'll find it almost everywhere you turn. Consider people like Judah, Ezra, the people of Nineveh, Nehemiah, David, and Anna—all were among those who sought God through fasting. As you read their stories, you'll find hope and divine expectation resounding louder than any noise your stomach could ever make.

WHAT ARE MY FASTING OPTIONS?

Fasts differ in all kinds of ways. The Bible records many different circumstances, types, and lengths of fasts. But the main three types of fasts found in Scripture are the *partial fast*, *normal fast*, and *absolute fast*.

A *partial fast* usually involves giving up particular food and drinks for an extended period of time. A partial fast can be interpreted many ways. The only way it cannot be interpreted is to include the time between about 11:00 p.m. and 6:00 a.m.—when you're sleeping!

The most commonly used example of a partial fast is found in the Book of Daniel. In the beginning of his captivity in Babylon, Daniel and his three companions refused to eat the choice meats and sweets from the king's table, asking instead to have only vegetables and water. They did this for ten days to prove that they'd be just as healthy as the king's men who ate meat and every delicacy. At the end of the fast they were vibrant and strong.

A *normal fast* is designed so you go without solid food of any kind for a certain length of time. You keep drinking water and plenty of it! Depending on the length of a normal fast, you may also choose to take in clear broth and juices in order to maintain your strength. Again, you'll want to talk to your parents (depending on your age) and a pastor before engaging in this kind of fast.

An *absolute fast* is an extreme fast that should be done only for very short periods of time. During an absolute fast you take in nothing—no food, no water. These kinds of fasts are nearly impossible without the grace of God. So you need to make 100 percent sure He is calling you to an extended absolute fast before you do it. Depending on your age, it may not be healthy to participate in an absolute fast. That's why it's important to talk to your parents or stepparents and pastor before ever trying an absolute fast. You should only consider an absolute fast with parental approval (depending on your age) and with medical consultation and supervision. Instead, consider one of the other options.

Before you decide which fast is best for you, take some time to talk to God and to older, wiser people, such as a spiritual mentor or church leader, who are passionate for the Lord and practice fasting themselves. They'll be able to guide you, offer encouragement, and give practical advice. Remember that the difficulty or length of the fast isn't what's most important—it's your heart before God and your willingness to seek Him above all else.

HOW LONG SHOULD I FAST?

The duration of fasts can vary. There are significant numbers we find in the Bible, which include three days, seven days, twenty-one days, and forty days. But there are also references to half-day fasts and twenty-four-hour fasts.

There's no real formula that I can give you to help determine which type or length of fast is right for you. The Bible is filled with different lengths of fasts. Later in his spiritual journey Dan-iel became grieved over the plight of Israel. In response he began another partial fast—taking no sweets, no meat, and no wine—for three weeks. He used the time to focus on prayer. At the end of those twenty-one days an angel answered his prayers. It's recorded that the apostle Paul was on at least two fasts: one for three days and one for fourteen days. Joshua fasted for forty days. Peter fasted three days, and, of course, we know that Jesus fasted forty days in the wilderness.

> "Is this not the fast that I have chosen: to loose the bonds of wickedness, to undo the heavy burdens, to let the oppressed go free, and that you break every yoke? Is it not to share your bread with the hungry, and that you bring to your house the poor who are cast out; when you see the naked, that you cover him, and not hide yourself from your own flesh?" —Isaiah 58:6–7

The length of your fast should depend on your age, circumstances, and health. You'll be amazed at the difference even a one-day partial or normal fast will make in your life. When I was a teenager, I started fasting for the first half of the day on Sunday. It made me so much more sensitive to the Lord. I'd notice more details in the sermon, find myself caught up in worship more readily, and even recognized God's voice more clearly in my life.

Again, don't bite off more than you can handle. There's no need to be heroic and attempt a forty-day fast your first time out. Just start. Once you discover the benefits, you'll be on your way to making it a lifelong practice.

At times the Lord may impress you to go on a longer fast. But for most people a twenty-four hour or a three-day fast is very practical. A "Daniel fast," eliminating meat, bread, and sweets for a set period of time, is a great way to start. Some may argue that eliminating only those three foods from your diet is no big deal. But if it means something to you, it will mean something to God. After all, when was the last time an angel was released to speak mysteries to you as one spoke to Daniel?

When I first started, I didn't start with twenty-one days. I just started with trying not to eat until after church on Sunday. Then I worked my up to a day, then three days. Eventually I built up to seven days and then to twenty-one days. What I've done recently is a total fast for seven days in January and then a total fast for three days each month from February to December. That's a total of forty days over the course of a year.

Remember that fasting should never put your body or your health at risk. On longer fasts I'll drink water, juice, and chicken broth when I need strength. Fasting isn't about feeling bad or weak; it's about making the time to be intentional about pursuing God.

A HANDFUL OF PRACTICAL TIPS

Over the years I've learned a lot of lessons about fasting—many of them the hard way. One of the biggest things I have to remember whenever I begin a fast is that if it doesn't mean anything to me, it won't mean anything to God. If I don't combine prayer and studying the Scripture when fasting, then going without food is little more than dieting.

The time apart from food is an opportunity to focus my attention on God. Fasting itself is a continual prayer before God. Now some days it just doesn't feel like that. Some days my energy is sapped, and I can't seem to focus in prayer. But there are other days when it feels like the heavens opened and my heart is prompted into deeper prayer.

Whatever I'm feeling, I need to remind myself that it's not about me. Fasting is about God. He sees the sacrifice, and He rewards those who seek Him.

I've also learned that, when fasting, your appearance should be normal. You shouldn't draw attention to the challenges of fasting through your actions, your treatment of others, or your temperament. Though your focus should be on your own needs, often God will stir the needs of others in your heart and make you aware of how you can pray for them or serve them.

> "Fasting does not only prevent sickness. If done correctly, fasting holds amazing healing benefits to those of us who suffer illness and disease. From colds and flu to heart disease, fasting is a mighty key to healing the body."
> —Don Colbert, MD[1]

When I start a fast, I often have a list of people I'm praying for, as well as one of my own concerns. But it's awesome to see how God grows the list of people to pray for as the fast continues.

Through the years I've also discovered that I need to be sure my heart is right when I fast. God said of Israel, "You cannot fast as you do today and expect your voice to be heard on high" (Isa. 58:4, NIV). What were they doing wrong? Israel was unrepentant and had forsaken the laws of God. Though they appeared to be seeking Him and delighting in His ways, their sin was all God could see. Instead of truly humbling themselves before God, fasting had become just another faithless mechanical performance—full of strife, anger, and lashing out. Fasting isn't just something to be done as if to check it off a list with God, but it's something that's to be done in humility and with a heart truly seeking after Him.

I've also learned that when I'm fasting I shouldn't sit in front of the television. My normal routine includes watching the news before going to bed. Once when I was on a twenty-one-day fast, Pizza Hut had just launched a huge advertising campaign for their new pan pizza.

During the newscast I'd watch as, during the commercials, images of a thick crust, meaty pizza slathered in bubbling cheese filled my television screen. Someone would dish out a piece of the deep pan pizza, and the melted cheese formed a hundred thin strings right before my eyes. My mouth gaped open. I could feel the crunch of the crust between my teeth. The pepperoni flavor filled my mouth. Suddenly I found myself thinking, "Where's the phone number for Pizza Hut?"

One night after watching one too many of those commercials, I dreamed I was eating a slice of pizza right out of the oven. The imagery was so real, I remember my conscience screaming, "This isn't right! Don't do it…you've only got another week to go!" But I stuffed it in my mouth and chewed and chewed. It was so good. I woke up a few minutes later, quite startled to find nearly half my pillowcase stuffed in my mouth.

Another lesson I've learned is that it's not a good idea to gorge yourself before a fast. I've been tempted to double up on meals a few days before a fast in hopes that I won't be as hungry. But all too often I end up hungrier during the fast. Instead, taper off your food intake in preparation for a fast.

FASTING CAN BE HEALTHY

People have been fasting for thousands of years. The Greek physician Hippocrates, who lived around 460–377 B.C., was known as the "father of modern medicine." His concepts have influenced the development of medical practices for centuries, and he was convinced fasting was good for the body.

Fasting is something like a spring-cleaning or a day at the spa for your body. When you choose not to eat food, this gives your body a chance to eliminate toxins. One of the ways many people can tell this is happening is that they'll notice a thin coating on their tongues for the first few days of a fast. Studies show that the average American consumes and assimilates around four pounds of chemical preservatives, coloring, stabilizers, flavorings, and other additives each year. These can build up in the body and lead to illness and disease. Period fasts give the body a chance to flush out these toxins and heal itself. In addition, fasting gives the digestive system a rest.

Regardless of the length of your fast, it's important to drink lots of water. I'm a big fan of trying to drink at least one gallon of water—filtered or purified if you have it—throughout the first day. Purified or distilled water flushes the toxins and the poison out of your system, which will help you get off to a good start. Plus, water makes you feel full. Water is fasting's best friend, so continue to drink plenty throughout your fast.

Water is also the great flushing agent in fasting. Another sign that toxins and poisons are being eliminated from our bodies can be seen by the concentration of toxins in our urine. These toxins can be as much ten times higher than normal when you're fasting. That explains why sometimes when you're fasting your urine may turn darker. The toxins in your body are being washed out.

I've also noticed as I've fasted that I often get a headache during the first day or two. That's often a sign that my body is getting rid of the toxins that have built up over time. As I said previously, fasting is like spring-cleaning for your body! It gives your whole digestive system a break, and that can be really healthy. After three days the headaches usually disappear for me. But if you're getting headaches, make sure you let someone know, and check in with a medical professional.

Fasting is challenging. When I've been on an extended fast, during the first few days as my body emptied itself of toxins, I didn't see angels or hear violins. In fact, I didn't feel much like focusing on prayer and the Word. But without fail, things soon cleared up, and I found a deeper place with God.

As your body is being flushed through fasting, all kinds of great health benefits can be experienced. For example, fasting is known to lower your blood pressure and can also lower your cholesterol—which is helpful for a lot of people.[2] It also has been proven that fasting sharpens your mental process and aids and improves your sight, hearing, taste, and all other sensory functions.

Fasting also breaks the addiction to junk food, which can so easily slip into all of our lives. I'm always amazed when just eating a handful of chips or a single cookie makes me start to want another and then another. If left unchecked, it's all too easy to look down and realize that I've eaten half (or all) of the bag. I'm sure I'm not the only one. Fasting helps break the power of an uncontrollable appetite. Some people find that freedom isn't just from food but other addictions including alcohol and drugs.[3]

Each year I encourage our church to join together in a twenty-one-day fast. Everyone participates in some way. They choose what kinds of foods they're going to fast from based on their age and health. Some choose to fast one day, others three days, some a week, and some even the full twenty-one days. As a congregation, when we all fast together over that twenty-one-day period, God is honored, and He rewards the sacrifice corporately and individually. At the end of those three weeks the stories are amazing. Testimonies of breakthrough, guidance, healing, and provision abound.

I've had people share that only *three days* into a fast for a loved one suffering with cancer, the person was completely cured. Another lady's son was dying from a 107-degree fever associated with his leukemia. The very first day of the fast the boy's fever broke, and he didn't suffer a trace of brain damage.

Though they both received miraculous rewards from God for their sacrifices, that was not enough for them. Both of them continued fasting for the twenty-one days. In fact, one of them continued for a full forty days. Not only did her son's cancer go into remission, but also the financial challenges she battled in her life were supernaturally broken.

Why weren't these people satisfied to fast just until they saw the breakthrough they needed in their lives? Fasting is not just a physical discipline; it can be a spiritual feast. Once you taste and see the Lord's goodness, your hunger for more of His presence eclipses the limitation of your understanding. God knows more about what you need than you do. All the fasts in the Bible—whether one day or forty days—brought reward.

And you don't have to be a certain age for God to do something miraculous. Jenna, a seventh grader, has done a twenty-one-day fast alongside her mother for several years now. She and her mom have been praying for one very important thing: that Jenna's older brother Brendan would come to know Christ. Brendan has been an alcoholic and drug abuser for many years. Despite his addiction, Jenna and her mom continued to invite him to church every Sunday and Wednesday. He refused.

But this last year as they were praying and fasting, they felt something was different—in a good way. They prayed that the Holy Spirit would convict Brendan of what he was doing and that God would draw his heart to Him. Two weeks into the fast Brendan asked if he could go to church with them. During the service the Holy Spirit convicted him, and he gave his heart to Christ. Now Brendan is telling the people he used to drink and do drugs with that, "Ya'll need this Jesus guy if you want to get your life right!"

If in twenty-one days you can be a new person or see the transformation in someone else's life—from the inside out, both physically and spiritually—why not consider giving it a try? Start with just a half day or a full day, but don't wait to take a radical step of faith. We have only one life to give to God—let's get control of our bodies and go for Him with the best we have!

Chapter 4

God's Assignment for You

W HEN I WAS a teenager, if you would have asked
me, "Do you plan to go on twenty-one-day fasts
throughout your life?", I would have responded,
"There's no way I could do that!"

But now I look back in awe at what God has done in and
through me since I embarked on the great adventure of fasting.
Just recently I completed my seventh twenty-one-day fast since
entering the ministry. I can't believe how far God has brought
me! I'm living proof that when you seek the Lord through
prayer and fasting, He gives you grace to do what you didn't
think was possible.

My parents were always godly examples to me. Even at a
young age I knew that fasting was an essential part of being
a follower of Christ. I started with shorter fasts. I'd give up
food until church was over. But eventually I grew to be able
to do one-, two-, and three-day fasts. In fact, it was during a
three-day fast that God revealed His assignment for my life. I
was praying and seeking His will. That's when He called me
to preach.

You see, God has assignments for us—things He has specifically called and created us to do. But how do you discover them?
How will you hear His voice? How will you know His will for

your life? His plans for you? Whom should you marry? Where should you live? What job should you take? What mission field is calling your name?

One of the best ways to seek God and hear His voice is through fasting. In my own life I've discovered that through fasting I solidified the assignment He has for me in my heart. And I don't think I'm the only one.

The apostle Paul made the following appeal to the Romans: "Present your bodies a living sacrifice, holy, acceptable to God, which is your reasonable service. And do not be conformed to this world, but be transformed by the renewing of your mind, *that you may prove what is that good and acceptable and perfect will of God*" (Rom. 12:1–2, emphasis added). That is how you "present" your body to God as a "living" sacrifice.

> "My sheep hear My voice, and I know them, and they follow Me. And I give them eternal life, and they shall never perish; neither shall anyone snatch them out of My hand."
> —John 10:27–28

I'm convinced that we'll never walk in the perfect will of God until we seek Him through fasting. When you present your body in this manner, you open yourself up to hear from the Lord. You will prove or discover His good and perfect will for your life. Paul was fasting when God called him and shared the assignment for his life (Acts 9:7–9). Peter was fasting on the rooftop when the Lord gave him a new revelation and called him to take the gospel to the Gentiles (Acts 10). They both received God's assignments in their lives through fasting.

Fasting prepares the way for God to give you fresh insights, spiritual awareness, and purpose.

One of the best examples of this comes from the Book of Joel. Now Joel was a minor prophet with a major message.

He was called to tell God's people that judgment was coming because of their refusal to walk in the Lord's ways. But Joel also predicted how God will save everyone who chooses to put their whole trust in Him.

The Lord says, "And it shall come to pass afterward that I will pour out My Spirit on all flesh; your sons and your daughters shall prophesy, your old men shall dream dreams, your young men shall see visions" (Joel 2:28). God was going to pour out revival—*afterward*. He was revealing His will for His people—*afterward*. After what? A fast. Israel was in sin, and the Lord called His people to fast in repentance: "Blow the trumpet in Zion, consecrate a *fast*, call a sacred assembly" (v. 15, emphasis added). God's promise to Israel was to pour out revival and blessings on the land after they turned from their sin. I don't know about you, but I'm ready for those *afterward* seasons when the Lord pours out revival, when we as the children of God are the sons and daughters who prophesy.

While studying the Bible recently, I stumbled on the importance of fasting in a passage I'd read many times before. In Mark's Gospel Jesus says, "No one puts new wine into old wineskins; or else the new wine bursts the wineskins, the wine is spilled, and the wineskins are ruined. But new wine must be put into new wineskins" (Mark 2:22). The principle is that we have to be transformed by the power of God in order to contain the fullness of God in our lives. We can't stay the same.

Though I'd studied this passage countless times, I'd never seen the connection between fasting and new wine before. But if you look at the context of the passage, you'll see that Jesus had just finished telling the Pharisees that His disciples would fast once He was gone (v. 20). In other words, fasting is what prepares you for a new anointing. God can't put His new wine, the kind of new thing He is doing, in old skins. If you want new wine, new miracles, new closeness, new intimacy with Him, then it's time to call a fast and shed that old skin for the new.

Fasting is a tremendous source of power available to anyone who wants to serve God more fully with their lives. His blessings in my life are a result of fasting. I'm not the greatest preacher; I don't have the brilliant mind of many, but God said He is no respecter of persons. When you honor and worship the Lord by presenting your body as a living sacrifice through fasting, you too will know His assignments for your life. I learned this many years ago when I was just a teenager, and it's just as true today as it was then.

SATAN HATES WHEN YOU FAST

Satan gets disturbed—and defeated—when you decide to be more than just a Sunday-morning Christian. The devil knows fasting releases God's power. Fasting helps you experience God's presence, receive breakthroughs in your life, and recognize your divine assignments. It's no wonder the enemy gets so upset.

Have you ever wondered why, of all things, Satan tempted Jesus at the end of His fast by provoking Him to turn stones into bread? Jesus certainly had the power to do so, but He came to use His power to serve others, not Himself. Furthermore, He was determined to complete the fast God had called Him to finish.

Jesus knew that some of the benefits of fasting couldn't be released otherwise—and so did the devil! When Jesus returned from that forty-day fast, He immediately began to do mighty miracles, "healing all who were oppressed by the devil" (Acts 10:38).

Remember, the enemy's agenda is to steal, kill, and destroy

you (John 10:10). Do you think Satan *wants* you to believe that nothing is impossible for you? He knows he is defeated, but he doesn't want you to know it or to walk in that realm of God's power. And he doesn't want you to know the Lord's assignment for your life or the incredible plans He has for you.

Don't allow the enemies in your life to cause you to focus more on your appetite or circumstances than on the divine promises that are released when you choose to fast and set apart your body, mind, and spirit to seek God.

> "For you were once darkness, but now you are light in the Lord. Walk as children of light (for the fruit of the Spirit is in all goodness, righteousness, and truth), finding out what is acceptable to the Lord." —Ephesians 5:8–10

Can you forgo that candy bar in the afternoon to be delivered from an area of struggle? To have more of the presence of Jesus in your life, can you drink water instead of sugary, caffeinated drinks for forty days? Will you set aside time to seek God and, in the process, rid yourself of all the doubt and confusion that fill your thoughts?

Like Jesus told the disciples at the well in Samaria, when you open yourself to know the will of the Father and do the will of the Father, no steak or cake compares. Nothing can fill you and satisfy you like that. Get ready for the presence of Jesus like you have never had it before.

Chapter 5

What If God Came to Dinner?

M Y MOM IS an excellent cook. She makes all kinds of delicious foods—salads, casseroles, baked breads, and melt-in-your mouth chocolate chip cookies. But imagine if instead of cooking a different meal every night, she only served one: meat loaf. Seven nights a week. Every week. For years.

I imagine that within a day or two someone in the family would have spoken up.

"Aw, Mom, meat loaf again?" someone would have complained.

If the days had rolled into weeks…then months…then years,

> "It is written, 'Man shall not live by bread alone, but by every word that proceeds from the mouth of God.'" —Matthew 4:4

I have a hunch that we all would have found a way to eat somewhere else.

But I think we can end up doing the same thing in our spiritual lives sometimes. We serve up meat loaf day after day and don't even realize we're doing it. Imagine that God is coming for dinner, and all we serve Him is the same dull religious routines day after day. Just like we would have complained about meat loaf on the table every night, I can just hear our heavenly Father sighing, "Aw, religion again?"

When we don't do what it takes to stay sharp and sensitive to the Holy Spirit, our praise, worship, offerings, and study of the Bible can become heartless routines to God. As a believer you can pray, study the Bible, and go to church week after week and still be losing sight of your first love. It's not that you don't love the Lord, but hectic schedules and a busy life can bring you to the point of losing your freshness, your enthusiasm, and your sensitivity to His Spirit and to what pleases Him.

That's why God said to Israel, "If I were hungry, I would not tell you; for the world is Mine, and all its fullness" (Ps. 50:12). The Lord owns the cattle on a thousand hills; He doesn't need our routines. He doesn't savor heartless activity. He doesn't want our "leftovers" when He can get "fed" elsewhere. True worship that comes from our hearts feeds Him and satisfies Him; it is something He desires—and deserves. Our religiosity of going through the motions once a week does not please Him as much as our obedience to His Word.

The reason this ties into the topic of fasting is simple: fasting is a constant means of renewing yourself spiritually. The discipline of fasting breaks you out of the world's routine. It's a form of worship—offering your body to God as a living sacrifice is both holy and pleasing to Him (Rom. 12:1). The discipline of fasting will humble you, remind you of your dependency on God, and bring you back to your first love. It causes the roots of your relationship with Jesus to go deeper.

AWAKENING TO GOD

God desires to move powerfully in your life. His plans for you are always progressing and developing. He desires to speak to you, as one would speak to a friend. That's how God spoke with Abraham. When the Lord came to judge the wickedness of Sodom and Gomorrah, He stopped by Abraham's tent on the way. Can you imagine looking outside one day and seeing the Lord walking up to your front door with two angels? Talk about out of the ordinary!

Abraham rushed to meet the Lord and bowed low to worship Him. He asked the three visitors to wait so he could bring water to wash their feet and prepare a meal. The three welcomed his invitation and stayed.

Abraham was a man who worshiped God, who spoke with God, and who had followed God's call to leave everything and follow Him to a land that He would show him. His worship and faithfulness had pleased the Lord for many years, and suddenly he had the opportunity to feed Him in a very practical way. The Bible says that after they ate, God told Abraham that he and Sarah

> "Do not be afraid, Abram. I am your shield, your exceedingly great reward."
> —Genesis 15:1

would have a son in a year. He even shared with Abraham His plans for Sodom and Gomorrah. Notice too that Abraham was then in a very intimate place with God in which he could intercede on behalf of the righteous who might be found in those wicked cities.

There are dimensions of our glorious King that will never be revealed to the casual, disinterested worshiper. There are walls of intercession that will never be scaled by dispassionate religious service. But when you take steps to break out of the ordinary and worship Him as He deserves, you will begin to see facets of God you never knew existed. He will begin to share things with you—about Himself, His plans, His desires for you—that are beyond your wildest imagination.

Another great example of a passionate worshiper from the Bible is King David. He was known to fast often. As a youth he was often in the fields alone with just the sheep and his God.

After he was anointed king, he spent many days running for his life from Saul.

David wrote Psalm 34 while alone and on the run from Saul in the land of the Philistines. Though he felt down and discouraged, David chose to worship God anyway. Surrounded by darkness and despair, he proclaims, "His praise shall continually be in my mouth" (v. 1), and "Taste and see that the LORD is good" (v. 8). A stale, unengaged worshiper in those circumstances might have been totally overwhelmed and ready to throw in the towel. But David knew the importance of worship—that we are created to give praise to God in all circumstances.

THE POWER OF MAGNIFICATION

David also discovered the principle that worshiping God magnifies Him. In other words, when we worship God, He becomes bigger—changing our perspective in life. The invitation of David to "magnify the LORD with me" (v. 3) still extends to us today.

When I was a kid, we didn't have toys like Xbox, PlayStation, or Wii. We just had simple toys and big imaginations to bring them to life. One of the best gifts my parents ever gave me was a large, handheld magnifying glass. It soon became an adventure waiting to happen!

I discovered that if I lined up the magnifying glass just right with the light of the sun, I could concentrate the heat from that light and burn a hole in a piece of trash or even toast an unsuspecting ant. And, of course, there was the main feature: the ability to enlarge anything you wanted to see.

When I held the magnifying glass up to an object, I saw things I couldn't see otherwise. I saw textures and details of everything from ants to my own fingerprints. Now magnification didn't make that object any bigger than it actually was, but it greatly enlarged my view, allowing me to see details that were hidden without the glass.

That's an important idea when we start looking at worship. Because sometimes in life your enemies or circumstances may seem so large and powerful they're all you can see. Maybe you have a friendship that has turned sour, or maybe you've had a falling out with one of your parents, stepparents, or siblings. Maybe you're looking at an impossible classroom or workplace situation. Maybe you're looking at a financial or health situation.

And. That. Is. All. You. Can. See.

But remember David's call to worship. When you choose to worship, you can't help but magnify God. Through worship He becomes bigger, and

> "If I were hungry, I would not tell you; for the world is Mine, and all its fullness. Will I eat the flesh of bulls, or drink the blood of goats? Offer to God thanksgiving, and pay your vows to the Most High. Call upon Me in the day of trouble; I will deliver you, and you shall glorify Me." —Psalm 50:12–15

the size and power of everything else becomes smaller. Worship "right-sizes" our perspective on life.

Later in Psalm 34 David wrote, "I sought the LORD, and He heard me, and delivered me from all my fears" (v. 4). Whenever you set your heart to worship God, He hears you. There isn't a word or a syllable that you offer up to Him that He doesn't hear. And when you magnify the Lord, you shrink the supposed power of your enemy, the devil. The greatest thing you can do when you're having a hard time is to magnify the Lord through worship.

The Gospel of John describes Jesus as taking a less traveled road. While the other religious leaders tried to avoid going through Samaria—even taking a longer route to avoid the town—Jesus trekked right into the heart of the region. Though Jews looked down on Samaritans and often avoided them at all costs, Jesus didn't hesitate. Entering the region, He decided to take a seat on top of a well in the heat of the day. Jesus sent His disciples into town for snacks and supplies. As He waited, a Samaritan woman approached the well. Jesus decided to ask her for some water. This may not seem like a big deal, but it bordered on scandalous. Jews didn't talk with Samaritans, and Jewish teachers didn't talk with women in public. Yet again Jesus didn't hesitate. He broke through the religious and cultural beliefs of the day.

The request for a cup of water became a doorway to a life-changing conversation. Jesus supernaturally revealed that the woman had been married many times and was living with a man who was not her husband. The woman's interest piqued. She wanted to know more.

She began quizzing Jesus about some popular religious issues of the day. One of her biggest concerns was about where to worship. Though she and her relatives routinely worshiped in Samaria, they had recently heard that the best place to worship was Jerusalem. Jesus explained that true worship isn't about a location. He explained, "True worshipers will worship the Father in spirit and truth; for the Father is seeking such to worship Him" (John 4:23).

As Jesus continued speaking to the woman, she became convinced she had found the Messiah—or, at least, that He had found her. She ran back to town and told everyone who would listen, "Come, see a man who told me all things that I ever did" (v. 29). The Bible says that the people of the town came out to see and hear Jesus—to worship Him.

In the meantime, the disciples returned with food, but Jesus said He wasn't hungry. They became worried that the Lord wasn't eating, but He explained, "I have food to eat of which you do not know.…My food is to do the will of Him who sent Me, and to finish His work" (vv. 32, 34).

While the disciples were busy gathering food, the Samaritan took time to worship Jesus and feed Him that which He most desired.

Consider for a moment what you're serving up for God in your own spiritual journey. Are you preparing a delicious offering of heartfelt praise and worship—offering yourself, your full self to God? Or are you serving up a stale and bland expression that feels meaningless, even to you?

Do you sense the Holy Spirit saying, "Aw, religion again?"

Or do you sense God's pleasure and joy as you spend time with Him and as He shares Himself with you?

Whatever you may be facing right now, I encourage you to answer David's call to magnify the Lord. If you are in a spiritual rut where you feel disconnected from God, if you haven't heard His voice or sensed His presence in a long time, if the challenges in your life are bigger than you can handle, consider starting to pursue Him through prayer, giving, and fasting. Don't wait another day to magnify the Lord through your passionate pursuit and worship of Him.

Chapter 6

You Shall Be Filled

H ave YOU EVER seen the television show *Man Versus Food?* For three years Adam Richman crisscrossed the country to compete in some of America's craziest food challenges. Each episode features the host trying to eat the impossible—foods that are impossibly large, impossibly hot, impossibly spicy, and impossibly fatty.

While the television show is entertaining (and a little disturbing at times), it illustrates a bigger trend that's going on in our country. People are overeating, and what we're putting in our bodies isn't always good for us. Much of the food is heavily processed and filled with sugar and preservatives. The result is that we're living in a day and age where people can eat large quantities of food, be overweight, and *still* be malnourished.

I think there's a parallel between our physical lives and our spiritual lives. We can become overnourished with food and yet malnourished with what our bodies really need. We also can become overnourished with religious practices yet be spiritually malnourished. We can fill up our lives with a healthy diet of gatherings and small groups and church services and activities—which can all be good things—but still live undernourished when it comes to the deeper things of God.

In the Sermon on the Mount Jesus told His followers,

"Blessed are those who hunger and thirst for righteousness, for they shall be filled" (Matt. 5:6). Jesus was saying that when you begin to develop a hunger for the deeper things of God, He will fill you. But hungering and thirsting for righteousness is more than attending a great young professionals, college, or youth conference or weekly service. Hungering and thirsting for righteousness goes beyond sitting in a chair in a church service for an hour or two a week. Hungering and thirsting for God means desiring more of Him in every area of your life. It means choosing to seek God through prayer, giving, and fasting. And finding the deepest longings of your heart satisfied in Him alone.

> "We may be actually starving from a nutritional standpoint, while at the same time becoming grossly obese....Sadly, we really are digging our graves with our forks and knives!"
> —Don Colbert, MD[1]

HUNGRY IN FLESH ... HUNGRY IN SPIRIT

While visiting the areas of Tyre and Sidon, Jesus encountered a woman who thirsted and hungered for God. She wasn't satisfied with a bare minimum faith. She was desperate for God.

This woman had a daughter who was possessed and tormented by an evil spirit. She tried everything she knew to get help for her daughter, but nothing worked. I imagine that on more mornings than she could count, she tried to hold her daughter to stop the thrashing and to silence the pain. Nothing worked.

Then the woman heard that Jesus was coming to town. She could have stayed home. She could have talked herself out of going to see Jesus—after all, she had already tried countless things that didn't work. And she was a Gentile—meaning she was not a Jew and therefore outside of the covenant God had made with Israel. But her spiritual hunger was too great. She had to go.

The woman didn't just ask for healing for her daughter once. She asked repeatedly. In response she received what in modern times would feel like a shrug from Jesus. The Lord explained that He wasn't interested in helping her because His attention was focused on the Jews. Jesus said the bread or fulfillment He was bringing was meant for the children of Israel, not for anyone else—not even for dogs gathered around the table. But the woman's hunger was so great, she refused to be discouraged. She persisted. She begged. She argued that even the little dogs under the table feed on the children's crumbs.

The woman's persistence and her answer stopped the Lord in His tracks. Jesus said that because of her answer, she should return to her daughter who had been healed (Mark 7:25–30).

Hungry people are desperate people, and they are hungry for more of God than they have ever had before. They realize that there's nothing to lose when it comes to pursuing Him. They are willing to take risks and be persistent in their relationship with God in order to lay hold of more of His presence, more of His power, more of His healing, and more of His miraculous work. Only Jesus satisfies that hunger.

Another biblical hero of mine who was driven by spiritual hunger to lay hold of the deeper things of God was a man by the name of Cornelius. Like the woman with the sick daughter, Cornelius was a Gentile. But that didn't stop him from passionately pursuing God. He and his household devoutly feared and served the Lord. He was a centurion, a man who led an army of about a hundred men. But his life was marked by the fact that he fasted regularly, prayed consistently, and gave generously to the poor.

One day Cornelius was fasting and praying when an angel appeared to him with a message. The angel said, "Your prayers and your alms have come up for a memorial before God" (Acts 10:4). Then the angel instructed him to send for Peter, who was nearby in the town of Joppa. Now it just so happened that Peter happened to be fasting at the exact same time. And while Cornelius saw an angel, Peter saw a vision. In his vision he watched as many foods that were unlawful for Jews to eat were presented to him.

> "While Peter thought about the vision, the Spirit said to him, 'Behold, three men are seeking you. Arise therefore, go down and go with them, doubting nothing; for I have sent them.' Then Peter went down to the men who had been sent to him from Cornelius, and said, 'Yes, I am he whom you seek. For what reason have you come?' And they said, 'Cornelius the centurion, a just man, one who fears God and has a good reputation among all the nation of the Jews, was divinely instructed by a holy angel to summon you to his house, and to hear words from you.' Then he invited them in and lodged them. On the next day Peter went away with them, and some brethren from Joppa accompanied him." —Acts 10:19–23

Peter was puzzled by the vision. Then Cornelius's messengers arrived. Peter traveled to Cornelius's house and spent time with him. As Cornelius and his family shared their passionate hunger for God, Peter and those with him realized that God was at work. Peter supernaturally understood the vision that he'd seen. The vision wasn't about food as much as it was about the gospel reaching the whole earth. The good news of Jesus wasn't just for the Jews but for everyone. As Peter shared the gospel with everyone at Cornelius's house, the Holy Spirit descended and baptized them all. Later they were baptized in water. (Read Acts 10 for more details on this amazing story.) Prayer and fasting played a crucial role in God revealing Himself to both Peter and Cornelius and brought salvation to many.

Fasting stirs a hunger in your spirit that goes deeper than any physical hunger you experience in your stomach. When you hunger for God, He will fill you. While Jesus's earthly ministry was filled with jaw-dropping miracles, it's worth noting that He didn't perform those "ooh-ahh" miracles everywhere He went. In fact, there were cities where Jesus traveled that He didn't perform any miracles because there wasn't any spiritual hunger. Even in the cities where He did travel and perform miracles, Jesus noted the lack of spiritual hunger and faith among some of the people. He also found spiritual hunger among the least suspecting people.

When Jesus entered Capernaum, a Roman centurion whose servant was paralyzed and tormented approached Him (Matt. 8:5–13). While many people wouldn't have been concerned with their servant's health, this man was very troubled. He did everything he knew to save his servant—including tracking down Jesus. This revealed his character as a leader, and it also showed that he was alive with spiritual hunger and vibrant with faith. He knew one word from Jesus would change everything.

When the centurion explained the situation, Jesus didn't hesitate. He promised to come and heal the servant. But the Roman centurion spoke up. He said he wasn't worthy for Jesus to come to his home. Instead, all Jesus needed to do was say the word, and his servant would be healed. As a military leader the centurion knew what it meant to be a man with authority. He knew that just as his soldiers did as he commanded, the evil spirits and sickness would do as Jesus commanded.

The Lord marveled at the centurion's response. He told His followers, "I have not found such great faith, not even in Israel!" (v. 10). In essence Jesus was saying, "Many in Abraham's lineage don't have the hunger this man has shown. They come to see Me, but they don't hunger."

I believe we're living in a time when God is looking for people who are spiritually hungry. His eyes are darting to the left and the right, searching for men and women who will long to go to the deeper places with Him. Will you walk among those who hunger and thirst for God?

GOING DEEPER WITH GOD

God honors those who hunger for Him and don't settle for living a spiritually malnourished life. Matthew 12:1–8 tells of a time when Jesus and the disciples were walking and talking together. The disciples became hungry. As they walked, they began to pluck heads of grain and scoop them into their mouths. But there was a problem. Picking grain on the Sabbath or day of rest was prohibited. On that day you weren't supposed to work or harvest any crops, but instead you were to choose to be devoted to the Lord.

When the Pharisees noticed the disciples plucking handfuls of wild grain, they protested to Jesus, "Your disciples are doing what is not lawful to do on the Sabbath" (v. 2). But the Pharisees had missed something amazing right before their eyes; namely, that they were walking and talking with the Son of God, who is the Lord of the Sabbath!

Jesus said to the Pharisees, "Have you not read what David did when he was hungry, he and those who were with him: how he entered the house of God and ate the showbread which was not lawful for him to eat, nor for those who were with him, but only for the priests? ... Yet I say to you that in this place there is

One greater than the temple. But if you had known what this means, 'I desire mercy and not sacrifice,' you would not have condemned the guiltless. For the Son of Man is Lord even of the Sabbath" (vv. 3–4, 6–8).

The Pharisees couldn't move past their own traditions to recognize that the Bread of Life stood before them. Satisfied with their own religion, they didn't hunger for the deeper things of God.

But when you hunger for more, you will receive more. Perhaps someone has told you, "You're too young," or "You'll grow out of that passionate zeal for God," or "With your background, God can't use you," or "Because you're a woman, you can't preach," or "You don't have the right 'connections' to do what you want to do." When you hunger for God and pursue His will, nothing is impossible.

Anyone can be normal. Normal is overrated. Someone in this generation has to say, "But I want more! Lord, I'm hungry for You." Will you be that person? Will you pursue God through prayer, study, giving, and fasting? Will you push aside your dinner plate every so often in order to chase after Him more fully?

Let's live in a way that shows we're desperate for God. Let's be filled with the Bread of Life each day. Begin to make fasting a regular discipline, and see how the Lord answers your hunger!

Chapter 7

Rewarded Openly

THERE'S NOTHING QUITE like sitting in the shade on the porch on a sunny day and drinking a glass of iced tea. You can watch the world go by. Friends and neighbors drive and bike past. You can see everything going on in the street—and everyone can see you. But when you're inside your home, you can't see out very well—and people can't see you. That's important to keep in mind when reading the words of the prophet Joel.

This Old Testament prophet instructed, "Let the priests, who minister to the LORD, weep between the porch and the altar" (Joel 2:17). On a house the "porch" is the part everybody can see; it represents the more public aspects of your ministry. The altar represents private ministry. And in your journey with God, you should always make sure there's more private ministry to God than public ministry.

In studying the life of Jesus, it becomes clear that He was more concerned with His private life with God than what everyone else could see. In fact, Jesus's private times with God shaped what He did in public—how He carried Himself, how He responded, and even the miracles He performed. This was particularly true of His prayer life. When you read about Jesus, you don't see Him praying in public nearly as much as you see

Him praying in private. The Bible says that Jesus often prayed through the night and engaged in intimate times of pursuing God while alone.

Out of those times in private devotion, public demonstrations of God's power poured out of Him in the form of healings, raising people from the dead, divine provision, and more. The miracles and victories of Jesus began in private. And we need to keep that in mind whenever we approach fasting. The practice of fasting—whether you're doing it on your own, with a group of friends, or as part of a church—is something that is meant to be kept primarily between you and God. While you'll want to let your pastor and family or a few friends know for encouragement and accountability, fasting isn't something to text all your friends about. You don't want to post that you're fasting on Facebook or take pictures for Pinterest. Why? Because where there's little private discipline, there's little public reward.

KEEP IT PERSONAL

Remember the threefold cord that highlights the duties of every Christian: giving, praying, and fasting. That teaching comes from the Sermon on the Mount found in Matthew 6. But if you keep reading the chapter, you'll discover that Jesus was concerned not only with what Christians do but also with how they do it. He instructed His followers not to perform acts of generosity or spiritual practices in front of everyone because if done that way, then there's no reward from God. Some people of the day actually sounded an instrument and made noise in order to let everyone know about their acts of generosity. Jesus called these people hypocrites. Instead of seeking the honor and glory of God, they wanted the honor and glory for themselves. Jesus says these people received their reward in full—the applause and pats on the back from people.

But if you want the smile of God on your life, if you really want to honor Him, then don't let lots of people know what you're doing. Trust that God sees you and that He will reward you—not just in private but also in public.

Whether done with a group of friends or church, fasting is mainly a personal, private discipline. It's a sacrifice born out of expectancy. That is not to imply that fasting is a manipulative tool to get something from God, but a "reasonable service" (Rom. 12:1) that He rewards openly.

God's rewards are often for all to see. Consider the life of Job. He went through

> "Take heed that you do not do your charitable deeds before men, to be seen by them. Otherwise you have no reward from your Father in heaven. Therefore, when you do a charitable deed, do not sound a trumpet before you as the hypocrites do in the synagogues and in the streets, that they may have glory from men. Assuredly, I say to you, they have their reward. But when you do a charitable deed, do not let your left hand know what your right hand is doing, that your charitable deed may be in secret; and your Father who sees in secret will Himself reward you openly." —Matthew 6:1–4

a devastating testing and trial and lost everything. His wealth, his family, and his health were all stripped away. Yet he prayed, he fasted, and he remained faithful to God. He kept on praying and talking to God. Even when he'd lost his family and wealth, he still said, "I have treasured the words of His mouth more than my necessary food" (Job 23:12).

And God blessed Job for his faithfulness. God restored Job's losses and gave him twice as much as he had before. The Bible also says that God blessed the latter days of Job's life even more than his beginning. Everything that was taken from him was replaced. He even had sons and daughters. God flooded Job's life with rewards for everyone to see so that he could be a living testimony of faith under trial.

In my own life I've asked for God to reveal to me how He wanted to openly reward the giving, praying, and fasting we were doing in our church community. I believe that what God showed me is available to everyone—even you.

One of the big things God loves to do when people pray and fast is bring them into a relationship with Himself. That's why it's important that as you fast, you target your unsaved loved ones in prayer. Consider creating a "hit list" of people you want to see saved. It's good to be very specific in your prayers during a fast. What is the one most critical thing you want the Lord to do in your life? God told Habakkuk to "write the vision and make it plain" (Hab. 2:2). I dare you to write down the names of those you want to see saved, and when you fast and pray, call those names out to God. I believe you too will see breakthroughs like you never dreamed of before.

> "And when you pray, you shall not be like the hypocrites. For they love to pray standing in the synagogues and on the corners of the streets, that they may be seen by men. Assuredly, I say to you, they have their reward. But you, when you pray, go into your room, and when you have shut your door, pray to your Father who is in the secret place; and your Father who sees in secret will reward you openly." —Matthew 6:5–6

I also felt God impress on me that, through fasting, He wants to bless people and remove any barriers created by poverty in their lives. That does not mean that you will fast from soft drinks for one day and fall into wealth. But if you begin to fast on a regular basis, and you begin to honor God with fasting, prayer, and giving, you will see for yourself that it is directly linked to poverty being removed from your life.

Did you know that Joseph, Daniel, and Solomon—the three wisest men in the Old Testament—were also the three wealthiest men? Joseph was forced to fast in prison. According to history, only the prisoner's family members were allowed to bring them food, and his family was in another country. But after that season of his life Joseph became fabulously wealthy and was put over all the money of Egypt (Gen. 41:39–45). Solomon humbled himself in fasting and in prayer, and God greatly increased his wealth and wisdom (1 Kings 3:10–13). Likewise, Daniel, who diligently sought God through fasting and prayer while in Babylonian captivity, was given wisdom over all the others and greatly prospered in the days of Darius the king (Dan. 6:1–4).

Earlier in the book I shared how fasting is a lot like springcleaning or a day at the spa for your body. Giving up food for a set period of time cleanses your body and gives your organs time to rest. But it's not just a physical spring-cleaning that's taking place. Fasting often increases our spiritual sensitivity to the Holy Spirit so that we're aware of areas of sin and compromise.

I've found that fasting isn't just humbling, but it also brings clarity. Often while I'm fasting, the Holy Spirit will illuminate any areas of unforgiveness and bitterness. That's a sign that God is at work as we set aside time to pray and fast. I know people who have tried repeatedly to forgive someone and haven't been able to let the matter go. But through a fast they've finally been able to forgive.

I've also sensed that, through fasting, the Lord wants to bring specific healings. A while back we were organizing our annual fast at our church. I felt the Lord saying that we were supposed to take a half- or full-page ad in the paper. We needed to invite people in the community as well as in our church to come and seek God's healing through prayer and fasting. Not only did we take out the ad and hold the service, but we also saw people healed from all kinds of diseases. When you fast and pray, you should *expect* miracles to follow.

You should also expect God to set people free—including you! If you have areas in your life where you've struggled with addiction or stealing or exaggerating or fantasizing or some other struggle, God wants to set you free. Sometimes the freedom will come during a fast, and sometimes it will come after.

One of my favorite stories is that of Manasseh, the son of Hezekiah, who became king of Judah (2 Chron. 33:1–13). Manasseh was a wicked man. God warned him many times to change his way of life, but Manasseh refused to listen. Then the army of Assyria captured Manasseh, put a hook in his nose, bound him in chains, and took him to Babylon. Manasseh could no longer ignore God.

It took a hook in his nose, but Manasseh finally gave in to God. He called out to Him through prayer and fasting. The Bible says God heard his plea and brought him back to Jerusalem into his kingdom. That's when Manasseh knew that the Lord was truly God.

Our Father longs to set His children free today, and He often does it through prayer and fasting. I've seen people with all kinds of hooks in their noses—pornography, alcohol, drugs, and many more—but none are stronger than the power of God.

One young gal I know, Kimberly, struggled with an eating disorder and suicidal thoughts. Through fasting for twenty-one days she experienced a powerful move of God. He not only healed her, but He also flipped the switch in her life and restored her completely. Kimberly's heart to serve, give, and to help others expanded greatly. Her eating disorder and suicidal thoughts disappeared as she realized God's plans for her. To this day she says, "Fasting and praying saved me and turned my life around completely."

One young man I know was a born-again, Spirit-filled fifteen-year-old when his dad committed suicide. He turned his back on God and ran hard and fast away from anything that had to do with Him. But God never gave up on him.

Shortly after he was married, the young man and his new bride stumbled back into church and sat in the balcony. At the end of his sermon the pastor gave an altar call asking people to commit their lives wholeheartedly to God. The young man tried to deafen his ears and turn away, but the Holy Spirit was vibrant in the moment. And the pastor was persistent. He kept calling people forward.

"The Holy Spirit won't let me stop," the pastor said. "He says there is someone here that if you don't take this opportunity today, you will never get another one."

The young man looked over at his new wife and said, "Well, are we going?"

Both of them went forward. The young man recommitted his life to Christ, and his wife accepted Jesus as her Lord and Savior for the first time. Raised Buddhist, she hadn't heard the good news of Jesus.

Now here's what's even more amazing! The young man's mother had been fasting for him and his wife to know Christ. Her fast ended ten days before they answered the altar call.

Fasting unleashes the power of God in our lives in ways that are beyond our earthly comprehension. But we can rest assured that "Your Father...will Himself reward you openly" (Matt. 6:4). What rewards does God have in store for you? How does

He want to use you to impact other people's lives? As you seek God through prayer, giving, and fasting, you can expect Him to do great things.

Chapter 8

The Power of Prayer and Fasting

W E PRACTICE FASTING regularly in our church. One of the most amazing things about a group of people coming together to fast is that you get to hear all kinds of awesome stories about the way God moves, speaks, delivers, and responds. Sometimes my heart is overwhelmed by the stories of people coming to know Christ, impossible healings, abundant provision, and the presence of God becoming more real in people's lives.

UNFORGETTABLE STORIES OF HOPE

I love the stories of how God brings people to a saving knowledge of Himself through fasting. One of those stories is Cheryl. She was fasting when her twenty-nine-year-old unsaved cousin Debbie called her out of the blue. Debbie was in trouble.

"We don't have to eat or anything," she said. "I just need to talk with you."

Debbie began to share with Cheryl about problems she was having in her life and relationships.

"The best thing you can do, Debbie, is to find a relationship with Jesus for yourself," Cheryl advised. "I don't know if you've ever prayed or accepted Him, but I can't leave here today without asking if you have ever been saved."

Debbie prayed with Cheryl and accepted Christ for the first time in her life.

Fasting makes you more sensitive to the timing and voice of the Holy Spirit. Even in the middle of the fast Cheryl had a boldness that she typically might not have had. Fasting does such a work in your life that the lost are often drawn to you and to what God is doing. It's not that we manipulate God through our works, forcing His hand. Fasting simply breaks you and brings your faith to a new level.

The stories of hope and transformation are found among those in our youth group. Jennifer, an eighth grader, recently shared that before our church's annual fast, she felt like her relationship with God was fading away. She had stopped praying, and it was difficult to hear His voice or feel His presence. Jennifer began to ask questions such as: "Why am I here?" "What is my purpose?" "Is God even real?" However, during the fast, she began to pray again, and her prayers were answered. She began to get involved in church and volunteer—even becoming a leader. Since the fast Jennifer says that the Lord has never been more real in her life. Such stories abound when God's people choose to seek Him through fasting and prayer.

I'm always inspired when I think of the story of Melissa. On the third day of her fast she shared the purpose of it: her dad was battling prostate cancer. That day her father went to the doctor for a procedure. To everyone's shock the cancer was gone. The Lord healed him. As a pursuer of God, Melissa didn't stop fasting when she heard the news. She kept right on going. She told me, "I'm going longer to see what else God wants to do." Her passionate love for Him shone brightly.

Melissa's story reminds me that God delights in rewarding His children. He is honored and magnified when we are willing to seek Him at all costs.

Another one of my favorite stories is of Susan. She worked for the same company for fifteen years, but she lost her job when another company bought them out. Then, without warning, her brother died in December, which left her sad and brokenhearted.

As I've mentioned, every January we have an annual fast in our church. And if anyone had reason to step back from the fast, it was Susan. But she bravely committed to fasting despite all the loss and pain in her life. Less than two months later her company called out of the blue and announced, "We're going to not only pay you an entire year's salary, but we're going to extend benefits to you for a full year." With the money her family was able to wipe out all their debt except for their mortgage, and they even purchasd a new vehicle. But the even bigger miracle was that as a result, God restored Susan's desire not just to live but to live the abundant life He called her to.

Another great story is of Darren and his wife, Sarah. They were told they couldn't have children. Despite the sad news, they chose to go on a twenty-one-day fast. Just a few months later Sarah was pregnant.

I smile every time I think of Joan, whose husband took the twenty-one-day challenge fast even thought he didn't know Jesus. Two weeks into the fast he woke up in the middle of the night crying. The next morning he gave his life to Christ and was baptized in the Holy Spirit. Not only did Joan's husband get saved on a twenty-one-day fast, but also, a few weeks later, her husband and all of her children were baptized. Joan loves to tell me, "To God be the glory!"

And then there's Lisa. Her son Ben was diagnosed with leukemia. He had gone through chemotherapy and had all kinds of terrible side effects. On January 5, the first Sunday we began the fast, Ben was lying in the intensive care unit, literally fighting for his life with a 107-degree fever. Knowing the severity of the situation, I announced at our church that we needed to begin fasting for Ben's recovery. Lisa told me that Ben awoke at that same moment and his fever broke. The leukemia eventually went into total remission.

Lisa's story doesn't stop there. She joined the twenty-one-day fast that year and continued on it for a full forty days. Lisa faced financial difficulties with a son battling leukemia, yet she still fasted for forty days. God heard her prayers. How do I know? The Holy Spirit spoke to a man and his wife in our church to buy Lisa a new van. I called her and asked if she could come by the church office, but I didn't tell her anything further. On her way there the car she was driving broke down. She arrived at the office and apologized for being late—with no idea what was about to happen. That's when I had the privilege of handing her the keys to a beautiful new van, complete with a DVD player for Ben to enjoy—and a check for an extra five thousand dollars from the couple.

> "I will praise the name of God with a song, and will magnify Him with thanksgiving. This also shall please the LORD better than an ox or bull, which has horns and hooves. The humble shall see this and be glad; and you who seek God, your hearts shall live." —Psalm 69:30–32

Several weeks later she shared her testimony at our church. Before the service I asked her how much debt she was in. She managed to pay off all her debts with the five-thousand-dollar gift, but she still owed twenty thousand dollars on her house. In that morning service I presented her with another check from that same couple, this time for twenty-five thousand dollars. Lisa and her son had lived their last year in poverty, thanks to a debt-free future and the open reward that God poured out on their sacrificial obedience.

One person I know in our church was hesitant to begin fasting. Twenty-one days seemed like forever. Then the person remembered that God rewards those who put Him first. At that time he and his wife had just one car and were living in an apartment. Over the course of the year, after the fast, he got another car. Then they moved into a house. As a musician, he soon learned that one of the artists he worked with landed a deal with one of the biggest labels in the world. He told me, "We'll fast again this year—and who knows?"

Another guy I know named Steve has a ministry where he goes into prisons and jails full-time. Despite his love for God, he really struggled with overeating. When anyone tried to bring up fasting in a conversation, he'd try to change the subject. But as our church's annual fast approached, he sensed the Holy Spirit working in his life. Steve knew he had an issue in his life to deal with—being consumed by food.

So he chose to go on a forty-day fast. "I didn't ask for God to open doors," Steve told me. "I told Him I was sick of gluttony cheating me out of the spiritual things He had for my life and locking doors and locking finances and locking everything else that He has for me."

Once Steve started fasting, he began seeing God open doors for him in every direction. He began getting invitations to share at more prisons. Television stations approached him to share about the ministry. One of the interviews was even with the same policeman who arrested Steve before he gave his life to the Lord.

I remember one year, at the end of the twenty-one-day fast, a couple walked up to me and handed me a bundle of official papers. Puzzled, I opened them up to see the word "Dismissed" stamped in bold black letters. After that I read the words, "The Superior Court of Gwinnett County, State of Georgia, Final Judgment and Decree of Divorce." The couple standing before me had been struggling in their marriage for a year, but during that fast, the season of setting everything else aside and diligently seeking God, a miracle happened. Unity replaced division, and the divorce was dismissed.

By this point I hope I've been able to clear up the misconceptions about what fasting is—and what it's not—and why it's a discipline that should not be missing in the life of any believer. Fasting is a vital part of that threefold cord of normal Christian duties that Jesus outlined in Matthew 6: giving, praying, and fasting. Setting time apart to go without food and seek God cleanses your body and promotes overall health. Fasting brings you into a deeper relationship with the Lord than what can be enjoyed through routine religion. And anyone can fast—no one is too young or too old. After all, Anna was a prophetess who was in her eighties when she worshiped day and night, fasting and praying (Luke 2:37).

As I mentioned earlier, if Jesus could have received what He needed to walk out His ministry here on earth without fasting, He would not have fasted. But He did fast; in fact, He has continued fasting for us for more than two thousand years. During His last meal with the disciples, He gave them the cup and said, "I will not drink of this fruit of the vine from now on until that day when I drink it new with you in My Father's kingdom" (Matt. 26:29). I have seen people who have never fasted before experience marvelous breakthroughs in their lives. If you are ready to bring supernatural blessings into your life and release the power of God to overcome any situation, begin today by making the discipline of fasting a part of your life. You will be greatly rewarded!

SECTION 2

Opening a Door to God's Promises

When the woman saw that the fruit of the tree was good for food...

—GENESIS 3:6, NIV

Why Is It So Hard?

I T'S STILL AMAZING to me that food was the enticement
used to cause Adam and Eve to sin, resulting in the fall
of mankind. I find it equally interesting that Jesus began
His earthly ministry—to redeem us from sin—by abstaining
from food.

I imagine it was an extraordinary sight for John the Baptist to
see his own cousin, the Lamb of God, descending into the water
to be baptized like everyone else. Most of the people who were
baptized that day probably went home afterward to celebrate
with a fine feast, talking about what they had seen and heard, but
Jesus didn't. He followed the leading of the Holy Spirit, beginning His earthly ministry alone, fasting for forty days and nights
while being tempted in the desert (Matt. 3:16–4:11).

The first thing Jesus felt in His earthly ministry was hunger.
The last thing He felt on this earth was thirst, as the Lord of
glory hung dying on a cruel cross (John 19:28).

So my question is this: Why do we as passionate
Christ-followers have such a hard time with the discipline of fasting? Lack of control over our appetites opened the door for sin's
temptation in the Garden of Eden, but Jesus took control over His
appetite, setting Himself apart in obedience to God, to break the
power of temptation. When Jesus fasted for forty days and nights,

Satan tempted Him to "command that these stones become bread" (Matt. 4:3). The enemy tried repeatedly to convince Jesus to focus on the desire for food rather than on the divine assignment from His Father, but Jesus knew that being set apart and walking in obedience were crucial to fulfilling His purpose on earth.

If Jesus needed to fast, how much greater is our need to fast? I was eighteen years old when I went on my first twenty-one-day fast. It was one of the most difficult things I had ever done. Fasting is never easy. Honestly, I don't know of anything more spiritually and physically challenging than fasting.

But I find comfort in knowing that Jesus understands. Hebrews 4:15 tells us, "For we do not have a High Priest who cannot sympathize with our weaknesses, but was in all points tempted as we are, yet without sin." In other words, Jesus knows exactly what we're going through. He understands what it's like to hear your stomach grumbling and feel it ache for food. But He also provides the grace that we need to seek Him through prayer and fasting. Verse 16 goes on to invite us, "Let us therefore come boldly to the throne of grace, that we may obtain mercy and find grace to help in time of need."

When you fast, you abstain from food for spiritual purposes. I've heard people say they were planning to fast their favorite television show or spending time on Facebook or unplug from Xbox or PlayStation. I think it's good and healthy to put those things down for a time—especially if they're interfering with your prayer life, your study of God's Word, or your ministering to the needs of others. But technically, giving up technology or entertainment isn't fasting. That's called abstaining. Fasting is choosing to go without food for a period of time. This creates an opportunity to step back from some of the busyness of life and choose to seek God through prayer, worship, giving, and Bible study.

Some people choose to fast for the wrong reasons. What are those? Well, some people think they can fast to earn credit with God—like getting brownie points. Other people think fasting will erase sin. But there's only one thing that will give us any merit or cleanse sin, and that's the blood of Christ—the sacrifice He made on the cross. Through Christ our relationship with God is made right again, and we have favor with Him as His children.

Some people also fast in order to lose weight. But fasting is not a Christian diet. You should not fast to lose weight, although weight loss is a common side effect. Unless you combine prayer with your fasting, there's no need to fast. Merely doing without food is just starving. Fasting calls us to focus on prayer and studying the Bible.

And some people fast so that other people will think more of them. They may fast to seem super-spiritual or closer to God. But fasting was never

> "Therefore do not worry, saying, 'What shall we eat?' or 'What shall we drink?' or 'What shall we wear?' For after all these things the Gentiles seek. For your heavenly Father knows that you need all these things. But seek first the kingdom of God and His righteousness, and all these things shall be added to you." —Matthew 6:31–33

meant as an opportunity to show off your spirituality. Rather it's an opportunity to focus on the needs of others. Some churches and schools have invited people to become more aware of the needs of others through a fast known as "Let it Growl," a world hunger and awareness fast. During this fast, when participants feel hunger pangs rise up and their stomachs begin to growl, they remember that one-third of the people in this world go to bed with that same feeling every night because they have no food.

Dr. David Yonggi Cho pastors the largest church in the world in Seoul, South Korea. The 750,000-member congregation goes on a twenty-one-day fast every year. He has 1,500 teenagers camp out on Prayer Mountain in tents to fast and pray for seven days each year. It's an amazing time.

As I've stated previously, God calls us to fast. In Matthew chapter 6, He names three things that Christians do: "When you pray…" "When you give…" and "When you fast." He didn't say "if" but "when." If you have a time to pray and a time to give, then you should have a time to fast. You can always find a reason not to fast, so when you make up your mind that you're going to do it, lean into God for His grace.

The first section of this book is called "The Private Discipline That Brings Public Reward." The "rewards" that have surfaced in the lives of those I know who fast have been phenomenal. In this second section I want to share some of the deeper teachings the Lord has given me on fasting, and I hope to encourage you with some of the magnificent stories of God's faithfulness.

Chapter 9

Be Pleasing to God

ASTING IS MORE exciting to me than ever. Don't get me wrong—I enjoy eating. True confession: it's hard to watch someone dig into a big, steaming, juicy steak while I'm chewing on steamed broccoli. But for me, hungering and thirsting for God brings with it a much greater reward than satisfying the temporary hunger I may be experiencing in my body.

I have a hunch this is something a woman in the Bible by the name of Anna experienced. The Gospel of Luke records just a handful of details about her life. In fact, she's only mentioned in three skinny verses. Though her story only fills a few lines, I believe God saw much more in the life of this precious saint.

> Now there was one, Anna, a prophetess, the daughter of Phanuel, of the tribe of Asher. She was of a great age, and had lived with a husband seven years from her virginity; and this woman was a widow of about eighty-four years, who did not depart from the temple, but served God with fastings and prayers night and day. And coming in that instant she gave thanks to the Lord, and spoke of Him to all those who looked for redemption in Jerusalem.
>
> —LUKE 2:36–38

As we see in these verses, Anna was known as a prophetess. She was also a widow, but she refused to allow her love of God to die along with her husband. Anna continued pursuing the Lord. She filled her days by praying and fasting in the temple. Anna had a hunger for God's Word that was greater than her hunger for food, and her faithfulness in fasting prepared her for what was about to happen next.

A young couple appeared at the temple. They were bringing their tiny infant there to be dedicated as their firstborn son. That couple was Joseph and Mary. They didn't stand out. No one recognized them or the treasure they were holding in their hands. They probably walked by hundreds of people in the crowded temple that day, but only one man and one faithful woman recognized the Messiah: Simeon and Anna. When Anna saw the infant, she began giving thanks to God. But she couldn't keep the secret to herself. She began telling everyone who would listen that the tiny baby was the long-awaited Messiah—the Savior of the world.

I'm inspired that, even as an elderly woman, Anna pursued God through prayer and fasting. I don't think fasting gets easier with age—so you can't tell yourself that if you wait, it's going to be better—but it does get better with grace. When the Holy Spirit nudges you to fast, rest assured that He's at work preparing you physically and spiritually for the days ahead.

BELIEVING GOD FOR EVERYTHING

Another person from the Bible who challenges and strengthens me as I continue to pursue God is Enoch. Like Anna, he's also one of those overlooked people from the Bible. The mention of him in Scripture is limited. But Genesis tells us his story: "Enoch lived sixty-five years, and begot Methuselah. After he begot Methuselah, Enoch walked with God three hundred years, and had sons and daughters. So all the days of Enoch were three hundred and sixty-five years. And Enoch walked with God; and he was not, for God took him" (Gen. 5:21–24).

I love those words: "Enoch walked with God." Not only did Enoch walk with God, but he also did it for three hundred years. His story was so inspiring that, thousands of years later, the writers of the New Testament were still talking about him. The Book of Jude records that Enoch prophesied in a manner that would have made him very unpopular with the party crowd (Jude 14–15). Enoch's primary concern was walking in faith, which is what pleased God.

> "I will lift up my eyes to the hills—from whence comes my help? My help comes from the LORD, who made heaven and earth. He will not allow your foot to be moved; He who keeps you will not slumber. Behold, He who keeps Israel shall neither slumber nor sleep." —Psalm 121:1–4

Even the Book of Hebrews talks about Enoch. The eleventh chapter is special in that it's often referred to as "the hall of faith." The chapter begins with the encouragement, "Now faith is the substance of things hoped for, the evidence of things not seen" (v. 1).

Many of the great men and women from throughout Scripture are highlighted, including Adam, and some of the most encouraging words in the Bible are found in Hebrews. The names read like a who's who: Abel, Seth, Noah, Abraham and Sarah, Joseph, and Moses. But do you know who else is included? Enoch. The Bible tells us, "By faith Enoch was taken away so that he did not see death, 'and was not found, because God had taken him'; for before he was taken he had this testimony, that he pleased God. But without faith it is impossible to please Him, for he who comes to God must believe that He is, and that He is a rewarder of those who diligently seek Him" (vv. 5–6).

What was it about Enoch that was different from those who went before him? What about his life was so pleasing to the Lord? Enoch came to God, he believed God, he diligently sought God, and he was rewarded. If you want to please God, *believe* God. Take Him at His Word. If I could choose what people say about me, I'd want my testimony to be like Enoch's.

HUNGER FOR THE WORD

Where does the kind of faith that enables you to look to God and believe His Word—no matter how challenging your cir cumstances may *appear*—come from? Your family may be facing some really tough times. You may have lost a close friend or family member and be trying to heal. You may be trying to further your education, and all you see are closed doors. You may be looking for a job and unable to find one. I could go on and on. These are very real circumstances that have no solution in the natural realm. Where does such faith come from?

> "Heaven and earth will pass away, but My words will by no means pass away."
> —Mark 13:31

In the Book of Romans, Paul tells us the secret source of faith: "So then faith comes by hearing, and hearing by the word of God" (Rom. 10:17). I like the Amplified Version of the Bible for this particular verse. It says, "Faith comes by hearing [what is told], and what is heard comes by the preaching [of the message that came from the lips] of Christ (the Messiah Himself)."

Faith is derived from hearing God's Word. Through study and listening to teachings on Scripture, faith naturally increases. Too many people live spiritually malnourished lives when it comes to the Bible. They live defeated lives as a result. Without a steady diet of the Scriptures they believe things that simply aren't true about themselves, others, or God.

Jesus gives us one of the best examples of the importance of really knowing what the Bible says. When He was fasting in the desert, the devil approached Him and tempted Him to eat. With each temptation Jesus answered the enemy with Scripture. He drew on a deep well of biblical knowledge in order to walk out His faithfulness to His heavenly Father. If Jesus turned to the Scriptures in trying times, how much more should you and I?

The Importance of Diligence

We must diligently feed on God's Word. Sometimes the best thing we can possibly do is starve our flesh and feed our spirit through a fast. Fasting helps you separate what you *want* from what you *need* by forcing you to focus on those things that really matter.

Believe me, fasting provides you with many opportunities to diligently seek the Lord! You diligently seek Him when everyone else is going out to the movies, enjoying sodas, popcorn, and licorice, and you choose to stay home to be with the Lord praying and fasting because you just *have* to hear from Him.

Diligently seeking God through prayer and fasting happens in the morning when everyone else gets up and eats bacon, eggs, pancakes, maple syrup, grits, hash browns, and fried sausage while you choose to spend time with God. It comes when you're at work and everyone else is having burgers, fries, and shakes for lunch, but you're having bottled water. Diligence is when you come home from a long, hard day at school or work, and all you've had all day is water, yet you separate yourself from the dinner table to feed on the Word.

To be diligent is to be persistent. Diligence means to work

hard in doing something and refusing to stop. God delivered the Israelites from Pharaoh's slavery. He parted the Red Sea so they could cross on dry ground, but He allowed Pharaoh's army to drown. Still, the children of Israel got out into the wilderness and started complaining. After all God had done for them, they weren't diligent about seeking Him, so that older generation didn't enter into His rest, His reward.

Faith is progressive. Faith never gets into a bad situation and says, "I'm just going to sit here and die. It's over." Faith never stands in the desert, having a pity party with everything drying up around it. You walk by faith. You don't stand still, drowning in your misery. When you get in a wilderness, you keep walking; you keep going forward even if you are only making an inch of progress with each step. When you get into battles, you have to keep saying, "I will move forward."

A GREAT REWARD

Have you ever seen the show *Dog the Bounty Hunter*? It features Duane "Dog" Chapman, who is famed for being the greatest bounty hunter in the world. During his twenty-seven-year career he has made more than six thousand captures. You may not know that he's a born-again Christian. Dog isn't just concerned with arresting the bad guys; he also encourages them to turn their lives around.

Now the whole process of setting a bounty on someone traces back more than a hundred years. In the Wild West, when outlaws rode on horseback causing all kinds of mayhem, the local sheriffs didn't have the resources, time, or energy to find and arrest them. So sheriffs put up "Wanted" posters offering a reward for capturing outlaws. The people who answered the ads were called "bounty hunters," and they spent their days tracking down the bad guys.

Fast-forward a hundred-plus years, and bounty hunters are still around. Today bounty hunters are professionals who are licensed, trained, and still play a crucial role in our justice system. Most of the time when someone is arrested, they get a chance to get out of jail by putting up bail money. If they can afford to hand over the money or have someone else who can afford it, they don't have to stay in prison until the trial. But some of these people skip town. That's where the bounty hunters come in; they track down the runaway in exchange for a percentage of the bail.

The thing I find fascinating about the whole process is that whenever a reward is offered for someone's capture, the reward is provided *before* it's claimed. The money is placed into an account where it's held secure until the offender is captured. That concept reminds me of our relationship with God. The Bible tells us that God is a rewarder of those who diligently seek Him (Heb. 11:6). That means He has *already* laid up rewards for you in heaven. What an amazing idea! God has rewards just waiting for you as you pursue Him with your whole mind, heart, spirit, and body. So don't wait. Begin pursuing Him today!

Chapter 10

The Garment of Praise

YOU NEVER FORGET the feeling of sorrow and loss that occurs when someone close to you dies. I loved my dad dearly. He was such a wonderful father, and his life was a celebration. I'm thankful that we had the opportunity to make so many wonderful memories together. When he passed away, I struggled to move beyond the initial impact of grief and mourning. Each day when I awoke, the sense of loss would hit me again as I thought, "My daddy is dead." But even though I knew my father was with the Lord, his absence left a void in me that took some time to heal fully.

> "To comfort all who mourn, to console those who mourn in Zion, to give them beauty for ashes, the oil of joy for mourning, the garment of praise for the spirit of heaviness; that they may be called trees of righteousness, the planting of the LORD, that He may be glorified." —Isaiah 61:2–3

I never saw the link between fasting and mourning until I was spending time reading the Gospel of Matthew. In chapter 9, a man by the name of John the Baptist asks Jesus a question. Now John the Baptist wasn't just Jesus's cousin, but he was also described as a forerunner to Jesus—a man who came before Christ to prepare the way for His earthly ministry. Prayer, fasting, and preaching marked John the Baptist's life.

One day some followers of John the Baptist approached Jesus and asked, "Why do we and the Pharisees fast often, but Your disciples do not fast?" (Matt. 9:14).

Jesus answered, "Can the friends of the bridegroom mourn as long as the bridegroom is with them? But the days will come when the bridegroom will be taken away from them, and then they will fast" (v. 15).

I found it fascinating that the words *mourn* and *fast* are used interchangeably in the Bible. The example the Lord gives in this passage makes it clear that fasting is much like mourning. When you are on a fast, you usually do not feel like celebrating. It's a time to press in to God, to seek Him, and to forsake the things of the flesh.

Reflecting on the passing of my father, I realized that I needed to mourn, and I also needed to fast and continue to pursue God. I found that He filled the void I was feeling with Himself. He brought healing and wholeness and a joy that's indescribable. How did He do it? Jesus said, "Blessed are those who mourn, for they shall be comforted" (Matt. 5:4). And I've discovered this to be true in my life. When we're going through difficult times, the Holy Spirit comforts us. He is the Comforter when we're mourning and when we're fasting.

When we fast, we get to experience the presence of the Holy Spirit in our lives in greater ways and discover how God wants to fulfill His promises in and through us. Though we may have been through hard times—even experienced things that left us feeling "burnt"—God wants to trade beauty for our ashes. He longs to give us the anointing of His presence, which is the oil of joy for mourning.

FASTING BREAKS THE SPIRIT OF HEAVINESS

Have you ever met anyone who is always down in the dumps? This person can always find the storm cloud even on the sunniest, blue-sky days. This person has a way of letting the air out of the balloons of life and turning what could be something awesome into a downer. A lot of times this person is weighed down by something I call a "spirit of heaviness."

A spirit of heaviness has to do with unhappiness, discouragement, and gloominess. Rather than seize the day and make the most out of every day God has for us, someone with a spirit of heaviness dampens the best of moods and the brightest of situations. Some people with a spirit of heaviness try to mask the pain by turning to alcohol, drugs, smoking, various addictions, or overeating.

Instead of looking for more stuff to put *into* one's body to ease the pain and

> "Then some came and told Jehoshaphat, saying, 'A great multitude is coming against you from beyond the sea, from Syria; and they are in Hazazon Tamar' (which is En Gedi). And Jehoshaphat feared, and set himself to seek the LORD, and proclaimed a fast throughout all Judah."
> —2 Chronicles 20:2–3

lift the discouragement, we should fast and seek God. He gives us a garment of praise to replace any unnecessary heaviness we may be carrying around in our lives.

What is the garment of praise? It's dressing or cloaking yourself in the joy that you're designed to experience as a child of God.

Instead of wearing the garment of praise, too many of us wear depression and oppression as if they were a garment shrouding us—and those around us—in darkness and despair. If you've ever felt the heaviness of discouragement or depression, then you know that it's hard to raise your hands to praise God in those moments.

That's why the garment of praise is so important. Just as you change your physical clothes, you can change your spiritual clothes. You can begin sporting the garment of praise. You can choose to worship and praise God—not just when you're at church but even on your own. And as you praise, you'll find heaviness lifting and joy filling your heart and life again.

> "So they rose early in the morning and went out into the Wilderness of Tekoa; and as they went out, Jehoshaphat stood and said, 'Hear me, O Judah and you inhabitants of Jerusalem: Believe in the LORD your God, and you shall be established; believe His prophets, and you shall prosper.' And when he had consulted with the people, he appointed those who should sing to the LORD, and who should praise the beauty of holiness, as they went out before the army and were saying: 'Praise the LORD, for His mercy endures forever.'" —2 Chronicles 20:20–21

One of my favorite examples of this fact is found in Second Chronicles. I shared a little bit of King Jehoshaphat's story in chapter 3. Now King Jehoshaphat had just gotten the kingdom of Judah in order. Things were going well. But no sooner did they start enjoying that peace when they heard that an army—far larger than they could defeat on their own—was already on its way.

Jehoshaphat could have died under that spirit of heaviness. The Scriptures say that he "feared," but he only paused a moment there. He immediately set himself and all the people of Judah to seek the Lord through fasting and prayer.

Then he took his place in the assembly of the people and began to praise—proclaiming who God was and all that He had done for them. The king ended by saying, "We have no power against this great multitude that is coming against us; nor do we know what to do, but our eyes are upon You" (2 Chron. 20:12). Then they waited.

How many times do we find ourselves saying that same thing: "I don't know what to do. This problem is far too big for me to handle."

God told them that the battle was not theirs but His. They would not have to fight this battle. He told them exactly where the enemy would be, and He also gave them specific instructions. They were to position themselves, stand still, and look for the salvation God would bring them. He told them not to fear or be dismayed.

I don't know about you, but realizing that the Lord was going to destroy my enemies would be reason enough to shout. And that's just what the people of Judah did. Young and old stood up and began praising God with loud voices. They began singing boldly in response to all He was going to do. The next day they went early to the place the Lord had directed them.

Then Jehoshaphat addressed the people again, instructing them to sing. As they sang and praised God, the Lord set ambushes against their enemies, and they were defeated.

There's immense power in praise—especially when it's coupled with fasting. Praise allows us to spin and dance with joy and thanksgiving for the goodness of God.

WHAT EATING ACCOMPLISHES

A friend called me just as our church was about to begin a fast.

"I feel so sorry for you," he said.

"Why?"

"Because you're going to give up food for so long," he said. "That sounds miserable."

"Don't feel sorry for me," I said. "I find incredible joy in fasting."

"What?" he asked.

"If anything, I feel sorry for you," I said, turning the tables on my friend. "I'll make a deal with you. Go ahead and eat food for the next twenty-one days. We'll compare notes at the end of the year to see if the food you ate accomplished for you what fasting for the next twenty-one days accomplished for me."

He agreed to the challenge, and at the end of the year when we compared notes, let's just say there was no comparison. I had seen so many miracles and God moments throughout the year; I couldn't even count them all.

> "That you may have a walk worthy of the Lord, fully pleasing Him, being fruitful in every good work and increasing in the knowledge of God; strengthened with all might, according to His glorious power, for all patience and longsuffering with joy; giving thanks to the Father who has qualified us to be partakers of the inheritance of the saints in the light." —Colossians 1:10–12

I'm awestruck by all the ways lives are changed when God's people fast. Jonathan is a ninth-grader I know whose sister had epilepsy. During a recent fast Jonathan's mom prayed for God to heal the epilepsy. When the fast was over, Jonathan's mom took his sister for a checkup. The doctor was astounded to discover the child had been completely healed.

But God was also at work in Jonathan's life through the fast. Raised by a single mom, he never had anyone to look up to as a father. But during the fast God revealed to him that He was his role model, mentor, and father.

I recently heard the story of a young couple who found out right after they were married that the wife was unable to have children. The couple tried medication, but the physician gave a slim chance for anything improving.

The couple decided to do a twenty-one day fast and seek God for physical healing. Each morning they took Communion and prayed together. They continued this throughout the fast. On the final day the wife decided on a whim to take a pregnancy test—she was pregnant.

Another recent example of the benefits of fasting is the transformation that took place in a young man's life I know, whom I'll call James. One Friday night my family and I attended a Christmas program at church and were driving home afterward. The forecast called for severe winter weather to hit over the weekend, so my wife, Cherise, asked me to stop by the grocery store to pick up some essentials. It was late, so I pulled up front and left the car running to keep my family warm.

I grabbed the milk, bread, and cereal and got in line to check out. I could see my kids watching me through the store windows. That's when I noticed him. A young man had entered the store right after I did and was now in line behind me holding a few cases of beer. I glanced back at him. Our eyes met for a split second.

At first I didn't think much about the incident because I was just grabbing milk and cereal. But remember, I had fasted for twenty-one days at the beginning of the year, and fasting makes you more sensitive to the voice of God. Suddenly in my spirit I heard the Lord say, "Tell him he has great worth to Me."

I looked back at the young man. He looked at me. Then he walked away. I went through the line and paid for my things, knowing I was supposed to say something to him. I didn't see him as I left, so I walked out to the car. When I opened the door, Cherise and all the girls were saying, "Daddy, Daddy! Look, look, look!" They showed me the camera they had brought to take pictures of the Christmas drama. But when I looked at the digital screen, they had taken pictures of the guy from the line.

"What's going on?" I asked.

My wife and kids had a bird's-eye view of this guy stealing beer and wine from the store. Not only that, but they also took pictures of him in the act! That's right, the same young man of whom God said, "He has great worth to Me." My heart sank. I had the chance to tell this young man that he had great worth to God, that he didn't have to continue living like he was living—defeated by the enemy and trapped under the weight of heaviness. I didn't obey God in the moment, and I felt terrible.

I confessed to my family that the Lord had spoken to my heart, but I didn't obey Him. I jumped out of the car and went back into the store. I looked frantically for the guy in the all of the aisles. Then I saw one of my daughters walking toward me. She explained the man had left out a different door.

When I walked outside and got in the car, Cherise said, "I think I know where he went."

"Where?" I asked.

"I think he went to the next supermarket down the street," she said.

"You think so?"

"I guarantee you he did. He's in a red Camaro."

"Let's go!"

We rode down to the next supermarket, and as we cruised through the parking lot, one of the girls shouted, "There's the red Camaro!"

I parked, jumped out of the car, and ran inside to look for him. I knew where to look: the beer aisle!

I spotted him with a cart filled to the top with cases of beer and wine. He had pushed it to the edge of the aisle where he could slip out behind the cash registers and ease outside with his stolen load.

But that wasn't God's plan for him! I walked right up to the young man and said, "You don't know me, and I don't know you, but God wants you to know that you have great worth to Him."

He stared at me for a moment. "What did you say?" he asked.

I reached in my pocket and pulled out all the cash I had— forty dollars.

"I know when I give you this money you're probably going to buy that alcohol with it, but I've got to obey God. And He told me to tell you, sir, you have great worth to Him, and He loves you."

"I can't believe this is happening. Who are you?"

"I'm a preacher."

"Where do you preach?"

"At Free Chapel over on McEver Road."

"Thank you," he said. "I can't, you know, I can't quit. I've been in six rehabs, and I can't quit."

Again I repeated what the Lord had spoken to my heart: this man was loved by God and had great worth in His eyes. In response the young man backed up two steps.

"Are you ready to walk out of here and leave it?" I asked.

He looked at me very seriously, paused for a moment, and then said, "Let's go!"

We walked to the parking lot together. The girls were all sitting in the car praying for this guy the whole time I was talking to him. He walked out wiping tears from his eyes. I put my arm around him and said, "You just need to ask Jesus to help you, son. He knows. He understands. He sent me during this Christmas season to tell you, 'You have great worth.'"

Everyone else, including the man himself, had said, "You're worthless. You'll never amount to anything. You're a failure. You've wasted your life." But God saw things differently. I prayed with that man in the parking lot, and we parted ways. The last thing he told me was, "I'll be at your church, Pastor."

I began to pray for him every day. Christmas came and went. New Year's came and went. We were a few days into our corporate fast when I saw him walking toward me one Sunday morning. He had a big smile on his face. He said, "I told you I'd be here." We started our year off with a miracle!

> "Now He who searches the hearts knows what the mind of the Spirit is, because He makes intercession for the saints according to the will of God. And we know that all things work together for good to those who love God, to those who are the called according to His purpose." —Romans 8:27–28

No matter what's going on in your life right now, you can set yourself to fasting and praying to seek God, who sees you as having great worth. Don't believe false truths about yourself. Don't sink further under the weight of heaviness. God has a garment of praise for you. His yoke is easy and His burden is light (Matt. 11:30). As you fast, you will begin to see yourself through His eyes—and you are of more worth to Him than you can imagine.

Chapter 11

Fasting, Faith, and Patience

DON'T KNOW WHAT grade I was in, but I can still remember an experiment my teacher had us perform. The teacher told us to save our milk cartons from lunch for a special event. She instructed us to bring them back to class, and then we'd rinse them. Afterward we cut off the awkward-shaped tops. Then she opened a huge bag of black potting soil, and we each scooped some into our cartons. She handed everyone a big butter bean seed and told us how to plant it in the soil by making a small hole with our finger and dropping in the seed. After I pressed the dirt back down into the hole, I watered the seed, taped my name to the box, and set it in the sunny window beside everyone else's.

Every day when that class started, I ran to the window with the other students to see what was happening with the seeds. We didn't see anything until the third day, when a tiny bit of green sprouted in some of the boxes. By day six, most of the boxes had green sprouts, and some even had leaves showing—but not mine. For six days I eagerly ran to the window to look at my box; there was nothing but dirt. I watered it just as everyone else did. It sat in the same sun that everyone else's did, but no sprout. I wondered if my seed was even still there.

On the seventh day I couldn't take it any longer. I arrived to class before anyone else and used my finger to dig around in the soil to see if my seed was still in the box. I pulled it out, and sure enough, it had begun to sprout. My teacher walked in about that time. When she saw what was in my dirty little fingers, she kindly explained that I really should have left it alone and just waited. Since I pulled the seed out of the soil too soon, I destroyed the harvest. She was right. All the other seeds grew strong and tall, and before long, they were filled with multiple pods of butter beans—far more than any one seed that was sown.

DON'T DIG IT UP!

Looking back, the experiment was simple enough, but it left an impression that I still carry with me. I think that little childhood experiment has stayed with me for so long because I've learned that we do the same thing in our spiritual lives. We get a word from the Lord—it's just a seed—but it gets planted deep in our hearts: "God is going to bless me. I'm highly favored of the Lord. God sees my need and will provide for me. He will protect my family and save my lost loved ones." The mountains you face seem so big, but you take that tiny seed of faith, plant it into that mountain, and wait.

Before long, impatience sets in. The mountains seem even bigger than they were before, and your seed isn't showing any sprouts—no matter what you do. Other people are seeing green shoots—they're being blessed—but your life looks like lifeless potting soil. You may begin to second-guess yourself, "Did I really hear from God?"—like my wondering if the seed was still in the carton. Discouragement may begin to settle in. You may be tempted to dig your fingers in the dirt in search of the seed. You may even grasp it and pull it out of the soil, but then—just as I did in my childhood experiment—you may destroy the promise of the work God wants to do.

This principle is especially true when it comes to fasting. I've heard people say they just couldn't make it past a day or so on a fast because they got discouraged. They listened to their hunger pangs instead of listening to the Holy Spirit. They quit the fast before they'd even really begun. That's the equivalent of reaching into the soil and pulling out the seed without giving it time to grow.

When a man brought his son to the disciples to deliver him from seizures, the disciples weren't able to help him. So he brought the boy to Jesus, asking the Lord to have mercy on his son. Jesus cast out the demon that tormented the boy, and he was healed. I can imagine how the disciples began to question themselves and each other. Later they asked Jesus why they could not cast it out. The Lord answered them, saying, "Because of your unbelief; for assuredly, I say to you, if you have faith as a mustard seed, you will say to this mountain, 'Move from here to there,' and it will move; and nothing will be impossible for you" (Matt. 17:20).

People facing major obstacles usually believe they need "great faith" to overcome them, but that isn't what Jesus said. He said "nothing" would be impossible to us—not if we had *great faith*, but if we had faith like the smallest seed.

Someone once sent me a mustard seed from Israel. Just to put things into perspective, a butter bean seed is about four hundred times bigger than a mustard seed, but it will yield only a small bush. On the other hand, a common mustard seed is only about one millimeter in diameter, and it grows into a small tree. The more common mustard plants are perennial, meaning they grow back year after year. Each time they grow back, they develop deeper root systems. If you tried to yank one of these trees out of the ground, the stems would break, but the roots would remain—and those roots would regenerate a new plant.

That is the type of faith we are to have! Jesus put the emphasis on the bigness of God, not the size of our faith. With only a tiny bit of faith, like a mustard seed, we can move mountains, and nothing will be impossible.

As Christians we need to stop measuring our faith by the size of the problem. Instead we need to start looking toward the greatness of God. We need to plant that seed of faith—no matter how small—into whatever mountain stands in our way and believe it will be moved, because Jesus said it would.

The Gospel of Matthew tells us that Jesus's disciples were crossing a body of water when a storm set in. To the disciples' surprise they saw someone walking on the water toward them. At first they thought it was a ghost. But when they heard the person's voice, they knew it was Jesus. Of all of the disciples, Peter was the most courageous in the moment. He asked Jesus to invite him to walk toward Him on the water.

A bit wobbly at first, Peter took his first step out of the boat toward Jesus. The other disciples were in awe. Then a gust of wind caught Peter off guard, and he became distracted. Fear set in. He began to sink. He cried out to the Lord to save him, and Jesus thrust out His hand to grab Peter's.

Then Jesus looked into Peter's eyes and said, "O you of little faith, why did you doubt?" (Matt. 14:31).

Sometimes people like to pick on Peter because he sank in the water. But he took more steps on water than anyone else I know. We can miss the importance of that phrase, "O you of little faith." If Peter, a man of little faith, walked on water, then imagine what God can do with someone whose faith grows by waiting patiently and staying focused on Him.

NOT BREAKING THROUGH?

There may be times when you're fasting and praying and standing in faith, yet you still don't sense that anything is happening. There's no "sprout" showing through the dirt. Remember the faith of those before you.

Throughout the history of the Christian church God has raised up men and women who were willing to dedicate their lives to Him and diligently seek Him through fasting and prayer. Long seasons of fasting are credited for launching such

> "I humbled myself with fasting; and my prayer would return to my own heart. I paced about as though he were my friend or brother; I bowed down heavily, as one who mourns for his mother." —Psalm 35:13–14

revivals as seen by Evan Roberts in Wales, who fasted and prayed for thirteen months for that country. Healing evangelists such as John Alexander Dowie, John G. Lake, Maria Woodworth-Etter, Smith Wigglesworth, and Kathryn Kuhlman all understood the tremendous power of faith in operation throughout their ministries. At times they all faced challenges and difficulties, but they remained patient and kept seeking God.

You may have an area of your life where you're not seeing a single sprout, let alone fruit. Be patient. Continue pursuing God. Spend time in praise and worship so you're not dragged down with discouragement. Remember, God gives you the garment of praise for the spirit of heaviness. Sometimes you won't feel like praying when you are fasting, but pray anyway. You'll be amazed how God will show up, and it will be like all of heaven has come down and glory has filled your soul.

Chapter 12

God's Priorities

FOR TEN YEARS and 236 episodes, the TV sitcom *Friends* became a focal point for millions in this country.[1] Many people felt like they were living life right alongside Rachel, Monica, Ross, Joey, Phoebe, and Chandler. Back when the show launched, critics described the series of six young single friends living in New York City as not very entertaining, clever, or original. The final episode had more

> "For if you live according to the flesh you will die; but if by the Spirit you put to death the deeds of the body, you will live." —Romans 8:13

than 52.5 million viewers.[2] The critics who said the show wouldn't make it didn't take into account the great need for relationships in all of our lives. We all crave connection.

God designed us to live in relationship with each other. We were made to live in community, not as lone rangers. But we need to keep a balance between being vertically and horizontally connected. We need to make sure we're pursuing God and pursuing healthy relationships—not just one or the other.

Fasting helps us become more attuned to God's call to love Him above all else and to love our neighbor. This doesn't mean that when you fast, you don't have specific needs and desires of your own for which you are seeking God. Indeed, you should fast for a specific purpose. But I believe that as you continue on a prolonged fast, the true cry of your heart becomes "more of You, God, and less of me" in every area of your life.

I want to show you several key aspects of life that we tend to get out of order. The apostle Paul wrote, "Now may the God of peace Himself sanctify you completely; and may your whole spirit, soul, and body be preserved blameless at the coming of our Lord Jesus Christ" (1 Thess. 5:23). Notice the order of Paul's words because they speak of God's priority in our lives. The Lord's concern is for your spirit first, your soul second, and your body third. But too often we get things backward by focusing on our physical needs or our bodies first and our spirits last.

We worry about things such as: "What brand should I be wearing?" "What will I eat for lunch today?" "What do I need to do to be accepted by others?" Jesus told us not to worry about such things, saying, "Is not life more than food and the body more than clothing?" (Matt. 6:25).

According to God's principle of "first things," what you put first will order the rest. When you put your spirit first, you serve the things of the Holy Spirit rather than the desires of your appetite. As a result your mind, will, and emotions, as well as your physical body and health, will fall in line according to the Spirit's leading. That's why I want to share with you some insights I've discovered regarding God's order of things.

FORGIVENESS

I heard a story once about a local woman who moved back to Georgia to purchase the old homestead on which she grew up. Her mother and father had passed away, and the land had to be claimed. One of the first things she had to do was hire someone to come clean out the well that her father dug many years before. Over the years a lot of stuff had accumulated in the well and made the water worthless.

The crew removed a good-sized pile of junk from the well and showed the woman so they could get paid for the job. But she said, "Nope. There's more in there. Please keep digging."

This went on for about three days. Finally, at the end of the third day, the woman looked at the latest pile of trash, toys, and miscellaneous objects that had found their home at the bottom of the well and said, "You're done."

Puzzled, one of the men asked how she knew that was it. She answered, "Because when I was a little girl and Papa first dug that well, I took a teapot and threw it in. I figured the first thing that went into that well would be the last thing that came out."

Fasting allows the Holy Spirit to come in, and just like those well diggers, He can begin to dig up the junk you've been holding on to without realizing it. When you begin to pray and fast, ask God to move deep in your heart through the Holy Spirit to expose any areas of bitterness, anger, or unforgiveness. Ask and keep asking. Look to see if there are any hidden teapots in your life. Maybe you have a

> "Now I know that the LORD saves His anointed; He will answer him from His holy heaven with the saving strength of His right hand. Some trust in chariots, and some in horses; but we will remember the name of the LORD our God. They have bowed down and fallen; but we have risen and stand upright." —Psalm 20:6–8

parent you've been harboring unforgiveness toward. Or maybe there's a friend who betrayed you or said something thoughtless online about you. Or maybe a boss or teacher has gotten under your skin.

When it comes to growing in our relationship with God, we need to understand the importance of forgiveness—not only the joy found in knowing that He forgives us but also that we are called to freely forgive others. This is crucial when it comes to prayer and fasting. While delivering His famous Sermon on the Mount, Jesus said, "If you bring your gift to the altar, and there remember that your brother has something against you, leave your gift there before the altar, and go your way. First be reconciled to your brother, and then come and offer your gift" (Matt. 5:23–24). Notice that Jesus says, "*First* be reconciled." That word *first* is huge! God desires our public and private worship, but before we can enter into the depths of prayer and praise, we need to perform a heart check and see if there are any areas of strife, contention, or unforgiveness in our lives.

Ask God to reveal any "junk" in your life, and wait to see what comes to mind. You may feel led to ask someone to forgive you for something you've done or left undone. Sometimes you may find there's a lot more than you ever guessed. But when you do get down to the deeper levels—the teapot level—and clean everything out, the river of living water can spring out of you and refresh others.

DISCOVERING GOD'S PRIORITIES

God's priorities are seldom our priorities. That's one of the big differences between the nature of humanity and the nature of God. He even said so: "For as the heavens are higher than the earth, so are My ways higher than your ways, and My thoughts than your thoughts" (Isa. 55:9).

How do you position yourself to hear from the Lord? How do you free yourself from your own desires in order to know His will? Well, I can tell you from firsthand experience that fasting causes you to take that sword of God's Word and separate what you "want" from what you "need."

The Book of Hebrews tells us the key: "Let us therefore be diligent to enter that rest, lest anyone fall according to the same example of disobedience. For the word of God is living and powerful, and sharper than any two-edged sword, piercing even to the division of soul and spirit, and of joints and marrow, and is a discerner of the thoughts and intents of the heart. And there is no creature hidden from His sight, but all things are naked and open to the eyes of Him to whom we must give account" (Heb. 4:11–13).

Did you notice the word *diligent*? Fasting, praying, and feeding on the Word of God puts that sword in your hand and positions you to discern the difference between your thoughts and His thoughts. Reading, studying, and memorizing Scripture will help you grow in your relationship with Him every time you do it because you're storing up God's Word in your life.

> "As for me and my house, we will serve the LORD."
> —Joshua 24:15

A man in our church is a pilot. Sometimes he lets me fly with him. He has taught me a few things about flying. The most crucial thing is to train yourself to rely on what the gauges in the plane tell you. When you fly a small plane into a storm, it will bounce in every direction. You cannot rely on what you feel. Your equilibrium gets out of balance, and you won't know if you're flying right-side up. The only thing that will take you safely through is relying on the gauges—relying on Scripture.

We need to learn to trust the reliability of Scripture when things get crazy. God's promises are your "gauges" when the storm of life rages. It's humbling to shut your mind off to what worldly wisdom and insight says is right and yield your trust to a few digital gauges on an airplane dashboard, but there's a lesson in that. The Book of James tells us, "But He gives more grace. Therefore He says: 'God resists the proud, but gives grace to the humble.' Therefore submit to God. Resist the devil and he will flee from you. Draw near to God and He will draw near to you. Cleanse your hands, you sinners; and purify your hearts, you double-minded. Lament and mourn and weep! Let your laughter be turned to mourning and your joy to gloom. Humble yourselves in the sight of the Lord, and He will lift you up" (James 4:6–10).

And as you study the Scripture, you'll find out what God's priorities are in your life.

Jesus said, "Therefore do not worry, saying, 'What shall we eat?' or 'What shall we drink?' or 'What shall we wear?' For after all these things the Gentiles seek. For your heavenly Father knows that you need all these things. But seek first the kingdom of God and His righteousness, and all these things shall be added to you" (Matt. 6:31–33). Again, fasting helps you to distinguish between what you want and what you really need. When you choose not to worry about these things and to seek Him first, you are demonstrating the kind of faith that is pleasing to God. You are trusting Him to also give you all the things you need.

YOUR LOVE FOR GOD

One of the amazing things that happens to me as I fast is that I renew my longing simply to be with Jesus. I find myself falling in love with God again. And this is one of His biggest priorities for us—that we would long for Him just as He longs for us.

How would you respond if the Lord asked you, "Do you remember the last time you were lovesick for Me?"

I spent some time thinking about this question. I thought back to when Cherise and I were dating. We were deeply in love and wanted to spend every moment together. It was probably a good thing our parents wouldn't let us because we surely would have starved to death. For the longest time, whenever we would go out to eat, she and I would end up taking about three bites of food because we were so engrossed with each other. I know that sounds silly, but stay with me—I have a point. I can't tell you the money I wasted on meals simply because

> "Walk about Zion, and go all around her. Count her towers; mark well her bulwarks; consider her palaces; that you may tell it to the generation following. For this is God, our God forever and ever; He will be our guide even to death." —Psalm 48:12–14

our desire to talk and spend time with each other was greater than our desire for food. We were "lovesick" for each other. As I thought back on that time in our relationship, it hit me. That's what the Lord feels when we fast. When we are so lovesick for our first love, God, then fasting becomes easy.

So I ask you, do you remember the last time you walked away from a meal because you were so preoccupied with your first love that the food was of no interest? Have you experienced seasons when it felt like God was distant? Maybe you just don't sense His presence as close as you once did. You have no heart for worship, and you lack the excitement and childlike enthusiasm you once had for spiritual things. Perhaps it's time to stop the busyness of your everyday life and declare a fast, a season of love-sickness to restore the passion of your first love back to its proper place. When you fast, everything slows down. The days seem to have more hours. The nights seem longer, but in the quietness of seeking, you will find Him whom your heart desires.

SOUL CLEANSING

Through prayer and fasting you're going to naturally become more sensitive to the Holy Spirit in your life. This should be a priority for all of us.

One of the characteristics of the Holy Spirit—which is true of God—is that He is holy. And God calls us to a life of holiness. Sometimes when you're setting aside time to pursue God in your life, you're going to find that the Holy Spirit is at work exposing things in your heart and life that aren't holy. You may find attitudes that are unbecoming. You may recognize comments that you thought were funny are actually hurtful and harmful. Or you may find that some of the thoughts that run through your mind are actually ruling your mind—and they're not God honoring.

Whenever you sense the Holy Spirit exposing one of these areas in your life, you can rest assured that these instances are born out of God's love. He longs for your holiness. He wants you to walk in holiness. God isn't just concerned with your outward behavior but with the inner recesses of your heart and spirit as well.

Jesus showed His concerns for people walking in holiness when He spoke some tough words to the Pharisees. He told them, "Woe to you, scribes and Pharisees, hypocrites! For you cleanse the outside of the cup and dish, but inside they are full of extortion and self-indulgence. Blind Pharisee, first cleanse the inside of the cup and dish, that the outside of them may be clean also" (Matt. 23:25–26).

The Pharisees had a double standard in their life. Though they said all the right things and taught all the right principles, they weren't living them out in their everyday lives. Though the Pharisees taught about God's laws, they lived their lives by finding every loophole and exception to the law rather than passionately pursuing a relationship with God. The result was that they were full of "junk" that needed to be cleaned out.

Before you're ready to perceive wrong in someone else's life, you first need to do a little self-examination of your own. You're worried about a tiny splinter in their eye when you have a telephone pole in your own. (See Matthew 7:3.) Hypocrisy is judging somebody else when there is something worse going on in you. Our attitude and lifestyle should be as Paul directed the church in Galatia: "Brethren, if a man is overtaken in any trespass, you who are spiritual restore such a one in a spirit of gentleness, considering yourself lest you also be tempted. Bear one another's burdens, and so fulfill the law of Christ. For if anyone thinks himself to be something, when he is nothing, he deceives himself" (Gal. 6:1–3).

That's why it's so important that, as you pray and fast, you take time to ask God to expose areas He wants to deal with or clean out. When you invite God to work inside of you, you're cleaning the inside of the cup so that the whole presentation becomes much more presentable.

> "Judge not, that you be not judged. For with what judgment you judge, you will be judged; and with the measure you use, it will be measured back to you. And why do you look at the speck in your brother's eye, but do not consider the plank in your own eye? Or how can you say to your brother, 'Let me remove the speck from your eye'; and look, a plank is in your own eye? Hypocrite! First remove the plank from your own eye, and then you will see clearly to remove the speck out of your brother's eye." —Matthew 7:1–5

GUIDANCE

In Psalm 23 God reveals Himself as a good shepherd. He wants to lead you and guide you. He wants to take you to the places at the proper time. Through fasting you can lean into God and discover His best for your life.

Remember the story of Ezra. After seventy years of Babylonian captivity he was about to lead the remnant of Israel—an entire generation of young people who had never seen the temple of Jerusalem, including some very small children—back to the Holy Land. It was going to be a treacherous journey home, but they had boasted of God's mighty hand of protection before heading out. So they had to act in faith and believe their own words.

Settled by the river, Ezra proclaimed a fast so that the people might humble themselves before God and seek His face. They needed to know the path they should take, for the protection of all who were with them.

One of the things God often does through a fast is provide direction and guidance. Sometimes when we're fasting, we need to know the right way to go in our lives because the choices and opportunities in front of us are confusing. Through fasting we can seek God and have confidence that He will guide us.

Maybe you have a question about whom you should date or marry. Maybe you're trying to figure out what to pursue in your education. Maybe you're struggling to figure out where to find a job or which one to take. The good news is that you don't have to be confused as you move forward in life. You can choose to seek God. A biblical fast provides an opportunity to set aside time to seek God for the right direction for your life. Examples are found in Judges 20:26 (Israel seeking to know if they should go into battle against the tribe of Benjamin), 1 Samuel 7:6 (seeking God at Mizpah for forgiveness and protection against the

Philistine army), and 2 Chronicles 20:3 (Jehoshaphat inquiring about the army that was about to attack).

GIVING YOURSELF WHOLLY TO GOD

One of God's priorities is found in the Book of Exodus. Moses instructed the Israelites, "And it shall be, when the LORD brings you into the land of the Canaanites, as He swore to you and your fathers, and gives it to you, that you shall set apart to the LORD all that open the womb, that is, every firstborn that comes from an animal which you have; the males shall be the LORD's" (Exod. 13:11–12).

This is an amazing text to me. Throughout Scripture God makes it clear that the firsts—firstlings of flocks, firstfruits of harvest, and firstborn males of families—all belong to Him. We are asked to give of our firsts, our very bests, to God. As you pray and fast, ask the Lord to reveal what areas of your life He wants you to give your firsts to Him. You may find the Holy Spirit asking you to give the first part of your day to God by spending time with Him. You may sense the Lord leading you to give the first portion of your paycheck to Him before you spend any of the money on other things. You may feel God leading you to give the first day of the month to prayer and fasting. Ask Him to speak to you about what "firsts" He is specifically calling you to give.

As you commit to prayer and fasting, you can look to God to be on the move in your life—revealing His priorities, igniting you with His love, cleansing you, making you holy, and revealing areas where you can give your first and best to Him. Be expectant.

Chapter 13

Ready for Battle

WHEN IT COMES to fasting, one of my biblical heroes is Daniel. Hel lived during the same time as the prophets Ezekiel and Jeremiah, which was a difficult time in the history of God's people. Why? Because the Israelites were being held captive in Babylon. Living far from their home, their culture, and everything else that was familiar, many of them began to struggle in their faith. Yet God raised up men—like Daniel and his friends—to remind the people of His power and the future He had for them.

Forcing an entire nation to move was no small feat. So when the Babylonians came into Jerusalem, they decided to make everyone move in three main stages. Among the first people they took with them were Daniel and his buddies Hananiah, Mishael, and Azariah—whom the Babylonians named Shadrach, Meshach, and Abed-nego. Why did the Babylonians take these guys first? Because they wanted to take the nobility; the people who were strong, smart, and good-looking; those who were at the head of the class.

When they arrived in Babylon, Daniel and his friends were forced to be prisoners in the court of King Nebuchadnezzar. You can imagine what a scary and harrowing transition this was for these young men. They probably wondered, "Where are we going? Will they let us live?" When they arrived at the king's court, they began to discover what was in store for them. They were to be trained for three years in the ways of the Chaldeans to eventually become the king's personal assistants. Having left everything—their homes and families—it may have been easy to allow their relationship with God to slip. But instead Daniel and his friends continued passionately pursuing the Lord and setting themselves apart from the others.

How did they do this? One of the big ways was by refusing to make themselves unclean by eating all the food laid out for them on the king's table. Instead Daniel spoke up to his chief officer, Aspenaz, and asked for permission not to eat the food.

> "Now God granted Daniel favor and compassion in the sight of the commander of the officials."
>
> —Daniel 1:9, NAS

Aspenaz really liked Daniel and wanted to help him, but he admitted that he was fearful of the king. If Daniel and his friends refused to eat and then looked worse, Aspenaz knew the king would cut off his head.

Daniel persisted. He asked Aspenaz to give them a chance. Daniel explained that he and his friends would be in better shape after ten days of eating only vegetables and drinking only water than the others would be after eating the king's delicacies. Aspenaz agreed to the test.

After the ten days the young men didn't just look as good as the others who ate everything—they actually looked better. Aspenaz agreed to feed them vegetables and water for the rest of their training.

As these young men continued to seek God, He gave them wisdom and the ability to learn. And Daniel received the divine gift of understanding other people's visions and dreams. At the end of the

three years Daniel and his friends stood before King Nebuchadnezzar. After talking with the young men, he determined that of all
the possible candidates to serve in the palace, none were as deserv-
ing as them. The king found that whenever an important issue
came up, there was no one better to talk to than these four men.

One day King Nebuchadnezzar had a disturbing dream.
Normally when the king had a dream, he'd share it with members of his court and ask for an interpretation. But after this
particular dream the king decided to demand an interpretation without ever telling them the details. On a whim King
Nebuchadnezzar announced that if no one told him the dream
and its interpretation, then he'd kill all the wise men in his service. When no one replied, he sent his men, including Arioch,
the commander of the king's guards, to kill all the wise men—
including Daniel and his friends.

When Arioch approached to kill him, Daniel asked, "Why
was there such a terrible punishment?" Arioch explained the
situation, and Daniel asked for an appointment with the king.
Then he went to his friends and asked them to pray. That night
God revealed the dream to Daniel, and the next day when he
met with the king, Daniel explained everything in detail. In
response the king fell facedown on the ground in front of Daniel and honored him. Daniel was showered with gifts and given
a promotion.

Throughout Daniel's life we get a glimpse of the power of
prayer and fasting. Over the years he continued to rise to greater
positions of responsibility and power—even with rulers other
than King Nebuchadnezzar.

When Daniel was nearly ninety years old, he received a
message from God that left him conflicted. In response Daniel continued pursuing the Lord. Scripture records, "In those
days I, Daniel, was mourning three full weeks. I ate no pleasant

food, no meat or wine came into my mouth" (Dan. 10:2–3). The Hebrew word used here for "pleasant food" is *lechem*, or breads. So for twenty-one days Daniel fasted from all sweets, breads, and meats, and he drank only water.

That fast is known as the Daniel fast and is probably one of the more common—with good reason. It's one of the partial fasts recorded in the Bible that brought with it great favor from the Lord. For twenty-one days he ate only vegetables and fruits and drank only water. In modern times that would mean killing the sodas, burgers, french fries, pizza, meats, sweets, and bread.

After three weeks of this limited diet Daniel was hanging out by the Tigris River when all of a sudden an angel appeared. Can you imagine having a conversation with not just any angel but one of the higher-ranking angels of God? Suppose that angel came to you and told you of kingdoms that would rise and fall in coming years, even explaining what principalities would manipulate those leaders and how alliances would form and be crushed as new kings rose to power. I'd be willing to give up a Twinkie or a T-bone steak for a few weeks in order to have my spirit open enough to receive such a visitation.

The angel told Daniel not to be afraid. Then the angel told him something amazing: his prayers had been heard in heaven from the very first day he started the fast (Dan. 10:12). The heavenly messenger explained that the only reason the angel had not appeared to Daniel sooner was because he was fighting with the principality of Persia. The passage is a powerful reminder that spiritual clashes take place all around us, and we don't even know they're happening. But as we pray and fast, we can trust that our prayers have an impact on the spiritual realm.

The apostle Paul echoes this idea of our prayer and fasting affecting the unseen spiritual world. In Ephesians 6 Paul challenges us to put on the armor of God so that we can take a stand against all of the enemy's schemes. He reminds us that the real struggle in our lives isn't against flesh and blood—the things we can see—but takes place in the invisible world, among the rulers and authorities in the heavenly realm. How do we battle those things we can't see? By dressing ourselves in the armor of God.

Paul advises, "Therefore put on the full armor of God, so that when the day of evil comes, you may be able to stand your ground, and after you have done everything, to stand. Stand firm then, with the belt of truth buckled around your waist, with the breastplate of righteousness in place, and with your feet fitted with the readiness that comes from the gospel of peace. In addition to all this, take up the shield of faith, with which you can extinguish all the flaming arrows of the evil one. Take the helmet of salvation and the sword of the Spirit, which is the word of God" (Eph. 6:13–17, NIV).

I love the imagery of the armor of God. We become covered with all the protective gear that we need to stand bravely and boldly with Him. We are protected so that we can hold our ground and also make advancements in God's kingdom.

Have you ever seen a military man try to fit into his uniform thirty years later? All too often the uniform won't even come close to buttoning down the front. But that's not how God wants us to live. When you're an enlisted soldier, you stay fit; you stay healthy, alert, and ready. And when you're serving God, you also need to stay fit, healthy, alert, and ready.

I want you to understand something: fasting and prayer sharpen the blade, which is the Word of God. When you fast, mealtimes often become study times. You become more keyed in to God's Word, and He begins to show you deeper truths. Notice that it wasn't after finishing off a box of chocolate-covered doughnuts that Daniel got the visit from the angel.

He began to understand God's truths after fasting and getting alone with Him. Understanding comes from the study of God's Word.

Many Christians have just stopped fighting altogether because they are battered and bruised or using dull blades. When you fast and pray, you effectively sharpen the Word in your mouth. Instead of flippantly quoting Scripture, you now wield a powerful weapon with a razor-sharp edge that slashes the enemy when you speak.

Amazing, isn't it? Simply by missing some meals and setting your heart on understanding by studying His Word, you please God and release beauty for ashes and joy for mourning. The garment of praise defeats the spirit of heaviness. Your praise goes forth and scatters the enemy, you develop patience, you come in line with God's priorities, you loose angelic messengers, and you find the Lord's right way for you.

LESSONS FROM NINEVEH

Nineveh was a great city whose roots trace all the way back to the Book of Genesis. Noah's great-grandson, Nimrod, actually started the city (Gen. 10:6–12). And despite his name, Nimrod must have been somewhat smart because the city he started became the biggest one in the ancient world.

In fact, the Bible states that Nineveh was so vast it took three days just to tour the city. Historians say Nineveh had walls 100 feet high with watchtowers that stretched another 100 feet. The walls were so thick that chariots could race on top of them. Surrounding the city of about 120,000 people was a vast moat 150 feet wide and 60 feet deep. Nineveh was proud, strong, and a popular place to be. And if any foreign army wanted to lay siege or attempted to surround and cut the city off, the inhabitants had enough supplies to hold out for at least twenty years. But Nineveh was filled with sin.

I want to stop there a moment and point something out. I'm sure not all the people of Nineveh were sinning. There were probably plenty of common, decent, God-fearing people. But remember what happened with Daniel in the last chapter. He had an incredible encounter with an angel after his twenty-one-day fast. Before the angel and before his fast, Daniel cried out to God on behalf of all of Israel. He kept saying over and over, "We have sinned and done wrong. We have been wicked and rebelled.…We have sinned against you" (Dan. 9:5, 11, NIV).

Notice that Daniel identified with the sin of his nation, though Scripture doesn't note that he committed any sin himself. The key is that he identified himself with the sins of the nation. Daniel didn't point at other people and their sin. Instead he recognized that he lived among them and approached God in humility on their behalf as one of them.

In the Book of Jonah we read about someone who wasn't as quick to identify with the sins of the people or have any compassion for them. God speaks to Jonah and instructs him to get up and go to Nineveh and preach against the evil things the people were doing. But rather than respond in obedience, Jonah hightails it in the opposite direction. He decides the best mode of transportation is a boat and sets sail for a place called Tarshish.

But God wasn't going to let Jonah turn down the divine assignment that easily. The Lord sent a storm on the sea that endangered everyone aboard the boat—until the crew discovered the real issue was Jonah. He was the one who had brought the storm on them. When the crew asked Jonah what they could do to bring calm waters back, he suggested they throw him overboard. And they did!

Then God sent a big fish to swallow Jonah. The rebellious prophet sat in the stomach of that stinky fish for three days before he was vomited back on shore. Jonah finally gave in to obeying God, but he kept a lousy attitude about it. He agreed to go preach a message of repentance, but secretly he hoped God would just destroy everyone in Nineveh.

After walking around Nineveh for a day, Jonah delivered one of the shortest and arguably least convincing sermons in the entire Bible. He told the people, "Yet forty days, and Nineveh shall be overthrown!" (Jon. 3:4). That's it. No explanation or argument. No compelling stories or altar call.

But then the most amazing thing happened: the people of Nineveh believed God. Illogically and miraculously the people chose to commit their lives to God. As a sign of their commitment and desire to pursue Him, they announced a fast. When the king of Nineveh heard the news, he was so moved he even issued a decree that no man or animal was to taste food or even water. Without any guarantee the king thought that by humbling themselves in this manner God may "turn and relent, and turn away from His fierce anger, so that we may not perish?" (Jon. 3:9).

God did turn from His anger and spared the city—despite Jonah's bad attitude. Though Jonah rebelled against God and tried to run away, God still got the glory and brought an entire city to the saving knowledge of Him. Despite this exceptional story, the later generations of Nineveh began to become more slack about their faith until they stopped seeking the Lord altogether.

About a hundred years later the prophet Nahum warned of judgment on the city: "The LORD has given a command concerning you [Nineveh]: 'Your name shall be perpetuated no longer. Out of the house of your gods I will cut off the carved image and the molded image. I will dig your grave, for you are vile'" (Nah. 1:14).

Nineveh, the capital city of Assyria, had lost their love of God and become cruel bullies who were more concerned with controlling the world than faithfully serving the Lord. The story is a powerful reminder that prayer and fasting isn't something just to be practiced once in your life but throughout your entire lifetime. You're designed and created for a relationship with God—to seek Him and know Him. Don't just plan on responding to God only in this moment, but respond in every moment as you faithfully commit your life to Him.

A HOLY DAY

Have you ever heard of the holiday Yom Kippur? It is perhaps the most celebrated holy day on the Jewish calendar. Yom Kippur means "Day of Atonement," and its roots trace all the way back to the Book of Leviticus. God established this holiday for his people. The Scriptures say, "This shall be a statute forever for you: In the seventh month, on the tenth day of the month, you shall afflict your souls, and do no work at all, whether a native of your own country or a stranger who dwells among you. For on that day the priest shall make atonement for you, to cleanse you, that you may be clean from all your sins before the LORD" (Lev. 16:29–30).

Notice the word *afflict*, which means fasting. Even Jews who typically do not observe any other Jewish festival will often participate in Yom Kippur by fasting, attending synagogue, and refraining from work to atone for sins against God. The Day of Atonement is the final day of "appeal" to God for cleansing, which is preceded by ten Days of Awe that are spent in reflection on one's life and sins.

On Yom Kippur in 1963, the nations of Egypt, Jordan, and Syria allied to attack and wipe out Israel. But the allied enemies of Israel picked the wrong day to attack. The entire country had been fasting and repenting of sin before God for twenty-four hours.

History records that the soldiers literally ran from the synagogues to the front lines, having had nothing to eat for an entire day. At first the battle was going toward the Arab armies who pushed Israel back for three days. It appeared that victory for Israel was impossible, but the battle turned on the third day. Even though they were significantly outnumbered, Israel's army was victorious and took back the ground they lost, plus even more.

Today when you hear news reports about things happening in the "occupied territories," remember that those are the additional lands Israel claimed in the Yom Kippur War. The enemy thinks you are weaker when you fast. He will try to convince you that you are dying without food—but you are not. God is preparing to breathe life into your situation to open a door to His promises.

CONTINUAL PRAYER

Fasting is not a means to promote yourself. The greatest thing fasting will do for you is break down all of the stuff that accumulates from this world that blocks you from clear communion with God.

Remember that fasting is meant to be coupled with prayer. You have to make time to get away and pray, whether you feel like it or not. Fasting in and of itself is a continual prayer to God. You are praying twenty-four hours a day when you're fasting. If you've been fasting all day, you've been praying all day.

Some of the greatest miracles, breakthroughs, and seasons of prayer I have ever experienced did not come when I was feeling led by the Holy Spirit to pray and fast. They actually came when the last thing I wanted to do was drag myself to my prayer place. But I did, and God honored my faithfulness. Jesus said, "When you pray...when you fast...when you give..." (Matt. 6). He expects those who follow Him to do these things whether they feel a special *leading* or not. These things should be part of every believer's life.

If you let it, your appetite will take over and rule your life. That's why times of fasting are so crucial to your walk with God. Fasting helps you establish dominion and authority over your flesh. "Do not be deceived, God is not mocked; for whatever a man sows, that he will also reap. For he who sows to his flesh will of the flesh reap corruption, but he who sows to the Spirit will of the Spirit reap everlasting life. And let us not grow weary while doing good, for in due season we shall reap if we do not lose heart" (Gal. 6:7–9). Keep your armor fit and your blade sharp!

Chapter 14

The Fruit of the Fast

F ASTING WILL PRODUCE lasting fruit in your life. As you pray and fast, you'll begin developing a greater appetite for the things of God. You'll also see miracles, break-throughs, and transformation happening in and around you.

I've found great encouragement about the lasting fruit of fasting in the Book of Isaiah. At one point the Israelites asked why they didn't get any response from God despite their prayer and fasting. In response the Lord told Isaiah why they fasted with no answer from Him. God called Isaiah to "cry aloud, spare not" (Isa. 58:1), telling the people to repent of their transgressions and fast the way God ordained. Isaiah goes on to tell the people what will happen when they do: "Then your light shall break forth like the morning, your healing shall spring forth speedily, and your righteousness shall go before you; the glory of the LORD shall be your rear guard. Then you shall call, and the LORD will answer; you shall cry, and He will say, 'Here I am'" (vv. 8–9). What awesome promises from God!

FULLY ILLUMINATED

I believe the promises Isaiah shared with the Israelites aren't just true for them but for us today as well. God wants to allow our light to shine bright like the morning. What does that mean? Remember that God is light. He spoke existence in the beginning of Creation, and according to the Book of Revelation, heaven won't need a single light switch because God is the source of all light. So when He promises to shine the morning light in us, it means He wants to illuminate us.

Remember the words of Jesus: "You are the light of the world. A city that is set on a hill cannot be hidden" (Matt. 5:14). God wants us to be luminaries—sources of His brightness in this world—and He promises to fill us with His light when we fast.

God intended Israel to be a "light" in darkness to other nations, glorifying their Creator by their actions and by His blessings being apparent in their lives. Naturally this draws others to God. Likewise, in our lives as children of God, our light will break forth and be apparent to others—I imagine much like the glow on the face of Moses when he descended from Mount Sinai after spending time with God (Exod. 34:29).

The stories of people's lives being illuminated as they fast are extraordinary. I recently heard from a woman who went on a forty-day fast from meat. She described that through fasting she heard God clearer than she'd ever heard Him before and that her life will never be the same as a result. That kind of transformation won't just impact her but also the people around her, because the light of God is shining through her.

HEALTH ABOUNDS

The second part of God's promise that Isaiah gave the people is, "Your healing shall spring forth speedily" (Isa. 58:8). Maybe you have a physical health issue or know someone who does. Or maybe you have another area of your life where you need healing. Through fasting God often works miraculous healings—some of them are beyond comprehension. I recently heard about a man who lost his bridgework (teeth) and couldn't find them anywhere. So he had a new bridge made and joined in the first of the year fast.

Somewhere around the fourteenth day of their fast, the man began to cough pretty severely. In fact, he got into such a coughing fit that he coughed up something solid—his original bridgework. This is a true story! Apparently, they had come loose in the night, and he had somehow inhaled them into his lung. (He must be a *really* deep sleeper!) It's one thing to be sick and be healed quickly. It's another for God to heal you of an issue before it makes you sick. If that bridgework had stayed in his lung much longer, he would have become very ill and required major surgery to have it removed.

Another awesome story comes from a woman who had protruding "knots" at the base of her spine. You could place your hand on her back and feel them easily. They caused severe, sometimes debilitating pain. She and her husband were part of our twenty-one-day fast at the beginning of the year. The first three days they went on a total fast, drinking only water, and then a Daniel fast for the remaining eighteen days.

On the second day her back was in major pain with no relief. She went over her prayer list, calling out the names of unsaved family members and other needs and asking the Lord to please heal her back. On the third day she was praying over her list and asking the Lord again to heal the knots. She placed her hand on them to lay hands on herself, only to find that they were gone. The woman had been completely healed on just the second day of her fast and had not even realized it.

Another story I got to watch unfold was from a nineteen-year-old man who had been diagnosed with cystic fibrosis at the age of five. He was admitted to the hospital because his oxygen level had fallen to 70 percent. His mom committed to fasting for him. About a week after the fast ended, he turned critical. His lungs could fail at any moment. People around his family committed to pray and fast for twenty-four hours.

On the twenty-third hour of the fast, the young man's carbon dioxide test came back normal. He was healed. His story reminds me once again that our God is beyond faithful.

Through fasting God often brings healing—not only to us but also to those around us. So as you pray and fast, ask the Lord whom you can pray for and be expectant for Him to do great things.

RICH IN RIGHTEOUSNESS

The third part of God's promise that Isaiah gave the people is, "Your righteousness shall go before you" (Isa. 58:8).

Your faith, your right standing with God, will cause you to move into areas where you would not have moved if you had not fasted. Doors will open to you that were not opened before, and your influence will go out like ripples in a pond. You'll find yourself more sensitive to the leading of the Holy Spirit and more prepared to respond in obedience.

Hunter, a thirteen-year-old, recently told me that before fasting this year, he had been messing up a lot in his life by hanging out with friends who were a bad influence. He was wrestling with the wrong stuff many teenagers deal with today. The peer pressure really started getting to him, and he gave in. But during the fast God showed Hunter that He had a plan for his life. Hunter began growing closer to the Lord and has kept on growing closer than ever before. He no longer hangs out with the bad influences and has developed healthy, strong relationships with people who are encouraging him to grow in God.

I recently had a woman write me and say, "I joined two friends in a twenty-one-day fast, after which the Holy Spirit delivered to me a special message about fasting. At His prodding I typed out the message and have shared it with others. Praise the Lord—the message touched hearts and helped others to understand the power of fasting. It is exciting to hear what God is doing in their lives because of their faithfulness to fast."

I mentioned earlier that when my brother and I started our first revival meetings many years ago, we took turns fasting. I would fast on the days he preached; he would fast the days I preached. We knew we had the right intentions in mind, but we were a little surprised when that two- or three-day revival lasted several weeks. We looked like half-starved refugees when the revival ended, but we had tapped into something powerful. I believe the doors that have been opened to me have been a direct result of His promises being fulfilled because of fasting. There are people whose lives can be forever made better because of your righteousness going forth with influence.

PROTECTED BY GOD

Most of us have heard the expression "I've got your back." It means that someone you trust is watching out for anything that may try to sneak up behind you and bring you harm. The fourth part of God's promise that Isaiah gave the people is, "The glory of the LORD shall be your rear guard" (Isa. 58:8).

In other words, when you fast, you can rest assured that God is providing for your safety in every direction. He's in front of us, drawing us toward a closer relationship with Himself. But He's also our rear guard, protecting us from attacks that we don't see coming.

Furthermore, God says, "No weapon formed against you shall

prosper, and every tongue which rises against you in judgment you shall condemn. This is the heritage of the servants of the LORD, and their righteousness is from Me" (Isa. 54:17). No wonder the devil wants fasting to remain the best-kept secret in the kingdom.

HE WILL HEAR AND ANSWER

The Israelites were fasting, but they were doing so with wrong motives, so they couldn't find God. But when we fast according to God's plan, He says, "Then you shall call, and the LORD will answer; you shall cry, and He will say, 'Here I am'" (Isa. 58:9). Remember what the angel told Daniel ? From the first day that Daniel began to fast, God heard. The only thing that held up his answer was a battle in the heavens (Dan. 10:12–13).

A woman I know recently gave a powerful testimony of this truth. Her parents had been in severe financial trouble for over a year. They had been given notice of foreclosure proceedings if they did not pay fifty-five hundred dollars. She called her unsaved brothers and asked them if they wanted to join her in doing something that would help her parents in their desperate situation. God backed her up. Her brothers agreed, and they began to fast. Within fifteen days of the house being foreclosed, her parents received a phone call. Her father had applied for disability in 2000, but it took six years for them to get around to holding the hearing on his case.

They called to inform the family that his disability application had been approved, and a check was in the mail that very day in the amount of—are you ready for this?—eighty-six thousand dollars, which included the retroactive amount from 2000. In addition, he would be getting disability payments monthly. There is no way her brothers can deny that God is the One who brought about this miracle.

God's promises don't stop there. If you go on to study the next verses that Isaiah spoke to the Israelites, He promises that as you care for others, "Then your light shall dawn in the darkness, and your darkness shall be as the noonday. The LORD will guide you continually, and satisfy your soul in drought, and strengthen your bones; You shall be like a watered garden, and like a spring of water, whose waters do not fail. Those from among you shall build the old waste places; you shall raise up the foundations of many generations; and you shall be called the Repairer of the Breach, The Restorer of Streets to Dwell In" (Isa. 58:10–12).

OBSCURITY AND DARKNESS

Your light will rise out of obscurity. In other words, in situations you face that are overwhelming and when you don't know how to find your way through the darkness of obscurity and confusion, God will cause your light to shine on the path you're to take.

My friend, Pastor Bob Rodgers, recently shared a great story with me. A man he knew lost his bakery business. Hard times hit, and the business went under just before the Christmas season. All he could afford to give his wife that year for Christmas was a seventy-five-cent card. In January he joined the twenty-one-day fast.

At the end of the fast he had an appointment to see his accountant in order to prepare his taxes and review the losses of

> "Is this not the fast that I have chosen: to loose the bonds of wickedness, to undo the heavy burdens, to let the oppressed go free, and that you break every yoke?" —Isaiah 58:6

the previous year. Now remember—he had fasted and sought God. When he arrived at the office, his accountant said, "I've been trying to call you, but your number has been disconnected. I heard about a man in Louisville who owns four bakeries. He wants to sell the businesses, and I thought about you. He wants to sell them for just twenty-five thousand dollars."

The man just kind of smirked and said, "I can't even afford to pay a twenty-five-dollar light bill right now. How can I come up with that kind of cash?" Still discouraged, the man left. On his way home he stopped at a stop sign. The white letters on the red background seemed more vivid than usual. While he was stopped, he sensed the Holy Spirit saying, "For twenty-one days you have asked Me to bless you, have you not? Turn back."

He immediately turned his car around and went back to ask for the name and number of the man selling the bakeries. Three men from his church gave him the money up front, and he was able to pay them back in full within six months. He could barely afford a card for his wife the Christmas before. At the end of their first year of giving their first days of the year to the Lord in fasting and prayer, he and his wife were so prosperous that she gave him an airplane for Christmas that year.

The Lord guided him back to His promise. That's another benefit of fasting: the Lord will guide you continually. Though the path before you may be obscure, when you fast and pray in faith, God will reward you and guide you. "Your ears shall hear a word behind you, saying, 'This is the way, walk in it'" (Isa. 30:21).

RAISE A FOUNDATION

Finally—and this is very close to my heart—when you fast, "you shall raise up the foundations of many generations" (Isa. 58:12). When you fast, you begin to lay a spiritual foundation that affects not only your life but also your future, including the generations that come after you.

I don't just fast for myself; I fast for my children, my future grandchildren, and so on. You're never too young to begin laying this kind of foundation for the future. I have laid a foundation through my devotion to God that He will build upon because He found an inroad to my family.

I recently heard from a woman who shared a remarkable testimony to this effect. She said that she did her first twenty-one-day fast after hearing me talk about the power of fasting. Here were the results:

"I believe the Lord told me I would be fasting for my sick father, who was not yet a believer. I felt I had a promise from God that my dad would not leave this earth without my knowing he is saved. Nearly three months after the fast, my dad died. But as the Lord promised, three days before his death, he assured me that he had asked Jesus into his heart.

"I also fasted for my twenty-two-year-old prodigal daughter, who walked away from the Lord when she was eighteen. I began this year with the twenty-one-day Daniel fast, again with my daughter as my focus. I recently heard from my daughter. She wanted to tell me that she is coming to church on Easter Sunday. It will be the first time in four and a half years. The Lord confirmed that this has occurred as a result of my fast. I am making fasting a discipline in my life."

Another person shared that after a twenty-one-day fast, she saw the hand of God over her and her family. She immediately noticed things were changing and moving like never before. She saw her son sober and in his right mind for the first time in many years. (He's thirty-five years old.) And she's expectant for all God will continue to do.

But fasting to raise a foundation isn't about praying just for those who'll come in future generations—but also those in your generation, including your parents and family members. A teenager named Reece recently shared with me that since he was in fourth grade, he had been the only one saved in his family. He grew up in a house where fighting and yelling were normal. Though his stepmom went to church a few times a year, his father didn't know God, and his brother was always getting into trouble. Reece decided to pursue God through prayer and fasting. He asked God to do something miraculous in his family. Within a few weeks his stepmom decided to start coming to church and has been attending every week since. Two weeks later Reece's brother and dad decided they wanted to attend too—and since then everything has been different in the family. There's no more fighting or yelling, and a renewed sense of peace has filled their house.

I love the way people's hearts soften toward the good news of Jesus Christ when people choose to fast. I sometimes wonder how many more people would be ushered into God's kingdom more quickly if more people fasted.

Chapter 15

Go for It

W HEN THE ISRAELITES left Egypt, God provided manna for them daily, as well as clothing and shoes that didn't wear out. Idolatry and unfaithfulness entered the hearts of the older generation, and they were left to wander in the wilderness for forty years. There was an entire generation that had grown up in the wilderness, listening to stories of the wonders that God had done to deliver Israel from Egyptian slavery—the plagues, the miracles, the plundering, the parting of the Red Sea, the drowning of Pharaoh's army, the fire by night and cloud by day, and the Ten Commandments written in stone. For nearly forty years they ate manna in the morning and manna in the evening while searching for the Promised Land flowing with milk and honey (Josh. 5:6).

Moses had been laid to rest. Joshua was now in charge, and things were changing. The command came from Joshua: "Sanctify yourselves, for tomorrow the LORD will do wonders among you" (Josh. 3:5). An extreme excitement must have spread through the camp, but the Lord would do wonders only if the children of Israel would sanctify themselves.

The Lord was about to lead His chosen people out against the enemies of God, but they couldn't stand if they weren't holy. The Hebrew root for "sanctify" is *qadhash*, which is also the root for holy. Leviticus 11:44 says, "For I am the LORD your God. You shall therefore consecrate yourselves, and you shall be holy; for I am holy. Neither shall you defile yourselves with any creeping thing that creeps on the earth."

Sanctification is the process of becoming holy in daily life; it's practicing purity and being set apart from the world and from sin. Sanctification is allowing the Holy Spirit to make us more like Jesus in what we do, what we think, and what we desire. We don't hear much about sanctification from the pulpit these days. But if we're to see God do wonders in our midst, we must confront sin in our lives and be holy.

KNOWING GOD'S WILL

Do you desire to be in the will of God and walk according to His plans for your life? Sanctification is the key to being in the Lord's will. The apostle Paul wrote, "For this is the will of God, your sanctification" (1 Thess. 4:3). There is no need to try to find some mysterious "wheel of God" out there. You can't follow the Lord's leading until you start where Paul said to start.

Fasting is an essential means of

> "For this is the will of God, your sanctification: that you should abstain from sexual immorality; that each of you should know how to possess his own vessel in sanctification and honor, not in passion of lust, like the Gentiles who do not know God; that no one should take advantage of and defraud his brother in this matter, because the Lord is the avenger of all such, as we also forewarned you and testified. For God did not call us to uncleanness, but in holiness. Therefore he who rejects this does not reject man, but God, who has also given us His Holy Spirit." —1 Thessalonians 4:3–8

sanctifying yourself, pulling yourself away from the world, and getting closer to God. Fasting allows you to filter your life and to set yourself apart to seek the Lord. Jesus prayed for us, "They are not of the world, just as I am not of the world. Sanctify them by Your truth. Your word is truth. As You sent Me into the world, I also have sent them into the world. And for their sakes I sanctify Myself, that they also may be sanctified by the truth" (John 17:16–19).

As I've shared, fasting will help you identify areas of hidden sin and things that are displeasing to God in your life. Fasting helps you discern between serving the flesh and serving the Spirit. "For if the blood of bulls and goats and the ashes of a heifer, sprinkling the unclean, sanctifies for the purifying of the flesh, how much more shall the blood of Christ, who through the eternal Spirit offered Himself without spot to God, cleanse your conscience from dead works to serve the living God?" (Heb. 9:13–14). If we are in Christ, His blood cleanses us from dead works, enabling us to serve God in holiness.

NECESSITY OF SANCTIFICATION

David was a man after God's heart, yet he cried out, "Create in me a clean heart, O God, and renew a steadfast spirit within me" (Ps. 51:10). We need a sanctification of *motives*. We need a sanctification of *desires*. We need a sanctification of *attitudes*. We need a sanctification of the *right spirit*. We need a sanctification of our *flesh*.

When we set ourselves apart for God, we find that complacency has no place in our life. We find pride, anger, bitterness, and unforgiveness vanishing from our lives. As we pursue God, He cleanses us from our sins and sets us free to seek Him even more.

The Book of Hebrews warns, "Beware, brethren, lest there be in any of you an evil heart of unbelief in departing from the living God; but exhort one another daily, while it is called 'Today,' lest any of you be hardened through the deceitfulness of sin" (Heb. 3:12–13). While the people leading your church should certainly set an example in personal sanctification and holy living, everyone is responsible for encouraging and exhorting fellow believers.

Exhort means to be abrasive with one another, to push one another to live holy lives so that no one falls into temptation and ends up turning away from God. Whom in your life can you be exhorting right now? Who do you know that needs an encouraging word? As you set yourself apart to seek God, He is going to bring these people to mind so He can pour out His love through you.

CROSSING OVER

Moses led the Israelites on a long, hot, dusty hike through the desert. Alongside him was a man named Joshua. Not only was he Moses's right-hand man, but he was also God's pick to lead the Israelites after Moses died. In the first chapter of the Book of Joshua God made extraordinary promises to His new leader. Not only did He promise to give the Promised Land to the Israelites, but He also promised that no one would be able to defeat Joshua throughout his life. God would remain with him through thick and thin.

As Joshua was about to cross the Jordan River into the Promised Land, he gave orders for the officers to command the children of Israel, saying: "When you see the ark of the covenant of the LORD your God, and the priests, the Levites, bearing it, then you shall set out from your place and go after it. Yet there shall be a space between you and it, about two thousand cubits by measure. Do not come near it, that you may know the way by which you must go, for you have not passed this way before" (Josh. 3:3–4).

The Israelites were to stand back and watch God. They were about to see the wonders they had heard about but never seen for themselves. As soon as the soles of their feet touched the water of the overflowing Jordan River, the waters separated just as they

> "Then the priests who bore the ark of the covenant of the LORD stood firm on dry ground in the midst of the Jordan; and all Israel crossed over on dry ground, until all the people had crossed completely over the Jordan." —Joshua 3:17

had in the Red Sea, allowing the new generation to pass through the waters on dry ground.

God stopped the river from flowing so that the Israelites could walk across safely on dry land. That's no small miracle. God wanted the people to know that, despite whatever challenges or opposition they would face in the Promised Land, He was with them. He even went before them and prepared a way. To help them remember the experience, God instructed the Israelites to pick up rocks from the bottom of the river and carry the rocks with them. Each time God's people saw one of those rocks, they would be reminded of the Lord's goodness and faithfulness.

That's a powerful image. When you fast and sanctify yourself unto God, it moves you off the bank and into the miracles. Why are the miracles of God so important? They strengthen our faith in Him and increase our trust in His ability to protect and provide. There are too many people on the edge of the shores of what God is doing and not enough of us standing firmly in the middle of His will. Do you want things to change in your home? You are the priest of your home—fast, sanctify yourself, and take a firm stance in the middle of God's will. No matter what your age—you're not too young.

When your family sees you stepping off the edge of mere "Sunday-morning religion" and getting right into the middle of what God is doing, they can't help but become more curious about Him and thirst to know more.

One of the other things that's important to notice about the Israelites' crossing of the Jordan River is that all the people of Israel crossed at the same place. I think that's representative of the idea that you need to be attached to a local body of believers. Don't try to make your way through life or the journey of faith on your own. We need each other. We need a spirit of togetherness, a spirit of trust, a spirit of unity, and a spirit of compassion for one another.

BLESSING OF SANCTIFICATION

Joshua's words went out to a generation chosen by God. Those who left Egypt didn't make it to the Promised Land—with the exception of Joshua and Caleb. They all passed away on the journey. Only the younger generation went on to inherit the promises of God. After everyone crossed the Jordan, the Lord instructed

> "Now the works of the flesh are evident, which are: adultery, fornication, uncleanness, lewdness, idolatry, sorcery, hatred, contentions, jealousies, outbursts of wrath, selfish ambitions, dissensions, heresies, envy, murders, drunkenness, revelries, and the like; of which I tell you beforehand, just as I also told you in time past, that those who practice such things will not inherit the kingdom of God." —Galatians 5:19–21

Joshua to "make flint knives for yourself, and circumcise the sons of Israel again the second time" (Josh. 5:2). The older generation was circumcised, but the younger generation had not been. They were to bear the mark of covenant in their flesh before God would take them any farther.

Circumcision speaks of sanctification of the flesh. It is cutting away dead things and hidden sins. You can look good publicly, raising your hands, giving your offerings, praying, and even fasting—but all the while hiding deadly sins. The blood of Jesus sanctifies you when you first accept Him as your Lord and Savior. But over time complacency and hidden sins can creep into your heart. You can start drifting, and you let your standard down.

The blessing of sanctification brings with it the promises of God's covenant and life in the Spirit: "But the fruit of the Spirit is love, joy, peace, longsuffering, kindness, goodness, faithfulness, gentleness, self-control. Against such there is no law. And those who are Christ's have crucified the flesh with its passions and desires. If we live in the Spirit, let us also walk in the Spirit. Let us not become conceited, provoking one another, envying one another" (Gal. 5:22–26).

What Is Your "It"?

More than twenty years ago when the Lord first called me to preach, He showed me some things that were for a time and season yet to come. I could not walk into all of His promises at once, but I knew He would lead me in His will as I was willing to sanctify myself and follow Him. Recently the Lord has stirred my spirit with a sense that now is the time. It's as if He's saying, "You've prayed about it. You've dreamed about it. You've asked Me for it. You've longed for it. It's been prophesied over you. Prepare yourself."

I recently traveled back to North Carolina, where I was born and raised. My grandfather still has a home in Middlesex,

North Carolina. It's a beautiful mansion-like homestead set on acres of rolling, lush farmland with horses, cattle, and even a private airstrip for his plane. Twenty-eight children were raised in that house over the years, and all of them serve the Lord.

During that special visit back to my roots, my heritage, I spent time each day walking that airstrip and the fields in prayer and communion with God. I felt the Holy Spirit's leading to visit the place down the road where He first called me to preach. I hadn't been back there in twenty-two years.

I went down to that wonderful old Church of God sanctuary and sat down in the very spot of my calling. I can remember like it was yesterday. I was on a three-day fast, and I was crying out, "O God, can You use me? Why are You calling me to preach? I can't do it. I don't know how to preach. I'm afraid. I'm not worthy. I'm not good enough." I was giving Him all the excuses and all the fear. I didn't realize that during the three-day fast I was cutting off the flesh with a sharp knife.

Finally, on the third day, I heard God's voice in my spirit say, "I've called you to preach. Go and do what I've called you to do." I said, "Lord, if this is truly Your will, then let my mother confirm it when I get home, even though it's past midnight. Let her be up and let her confirm it."

I was young, and it never hurts to ask for clarity. I walked out of that tiny sanctuary weeping, got into my car, and drove barely a quarter mile home. When I walked back to Mom's bedroom, she was on her knees praying. As soon as I saw her, she whirled around, pointed her finger, and started speaking with stammering lips: "Jentezen, God has called you to preach. Go and do what He has called you to do."

Sitting in that very same spot more than twenty years later, I was overwhelmed. Emotions like I've never felt before in my life washed over me. In that moment I again sensed the leading of the Spirit in my heart directing me to fast and sanctify myself a second time because He had prophetically led me back to that spot where I started. He was about to begin a new thing in my life. As God said to the children of Israel, it was as if He said to me, "You've never been this way before."

WHAT ABOUT YOU?

What if you set yourself to diligently seek the Lord, sanctifying yourself with a fast, and journey back to the spot where it all began—where He saved you, set you free, filled you with His Spirit, and called you out? I actually physically traveled to that spot. But if you can't do that, you can go back mentally. You can recall the ancient landmark, that same simplicity, innocence, and dedication with which you first responded to His voice.

God wants you to ask Him for—believe Him for—things that are bigger than yourself. I'm now almost fifty years old, but I can't just float through life. I can't kick back and wait for later. Too much is promised! I want to reap the harvest.

The children of Israel had made it through the wilderness. They had stopped eating manna and had begun to eat the good fruit of the land. They lived along a river, and they could have easily set up trade with those from the big city of Jericho, but that was not their destiny.

Fasting will bring you into your destiny. Fasting will bring you into alignment with God's plan for your life. Just as Joshua called the children of promise to sanctify themselves, I believe that, likewise, your "tomorrow" is just around the corner. God is going to do wonders in your life, leading you to places you've never been before. Now is the time to fast, to seek God diligently, to sanctify yourself, to discern God's priorities, and to walk in His promises. *Go for it!*

Notes

CHAPTER 2
KING STOMACH'S REIGN

1. *Matthew Henry's Commentary*, "Numbers 11," http://
www.htmlbible.com/kjv30/henry/H04C011.htm (accessed
April 13, 2012).

CHAPTER 3
BUT HOW DO I FAST?

1. Don Colbert, MD, *Toxic Relief*, revised and expanded
(Lake Mary, FL: Siloam, 2012), 149.

2. Ibid., 65, 153.

3. Ibid., 172–173.

CHAPTER 6
YOU SHALL BE FILLED

1. Colbert, *Toxic Relief*, revised and expanded, 37.

CHAPTER 12
GOD'S PRIORITIES

1. NumberOf.net, "Number of Friends Episodes," April 10,
2010, http://www.numberof.net/number-of-friends-episodes/
(accessed April 24, 2012).

2. Bill Carter, "'Friends' Finale's Audience Is the Fourth
Biggest Ever," *New York Times*, May 8, 2004, http://www
.nytimes.com/2004/05/08/arts/friends-finale-s-audience-is
-the-fourth-biggest-ever.html (accessed April 24, 2012).

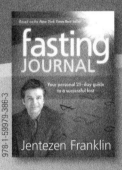

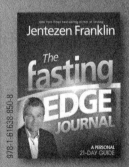

PASSIO

PASSIONATE. AUTHENTIC. MISSIONAL.

Passio brings you books, e-books, and other media from innovative voices on topics from missional living to a deeper relationship with God.

Take a look at Passio's other releases at the links below and ignite your faith and spiritual passion.

www.passiofaith.com
www.twitter.com/passiofaith
www.facebook.com/passiofaith